STOICISM FOR ENTREPRENEURS

How to Model Todays Best Entrepreneurs by Using the Ancient Stoic Self Disciplined Mindset

Joel E. Winston

© **Copyright 2019 - All rights reserved.**

The content contained within this book may not be reproduced, duplicated or transmitted without direct written permission from the author or the publisher.

Under no circumstances will any blame or legal responsibility be held against the publisher, or author, for any damages, reparation, or monetary loss due to the information contained within this book. Either directly or indirectly.

Legal Notice:

This book is copyright protected. This book is only for personal use. You cannot amend, distribute, sell, use, quote or paraphrase any part, or the content within this book, without the consent of the author or publisher.

Disclaimer Notice:

Please note the information contained within this document is for educational and entertainment purposes only. All effort has been executed to present accurate, up to date, and reliable, complete information. No warranties of any kind are declared or implied. Readers acknowledge that the author is not engaging in the rendering of legal, financial, medical or professional advice. The content within this book has been derived from various sources. Please consult a licensed professional before attempting any techniques outlined in this book.

By reading this document, the reader agrees that under no circumstances is the author responsible for any losses, direct or indirect, which are incurred as a result of the use of the information contained within this document, including, but not limited to, — errors, omissions, or inaccuracies.

How to get the most from this book

We live in a stressful and fast-paced world.

When reading a book, everything seems logical and clear, but after reading it, we tend to forget quickly and move on as usual.

We forget things, because we have to process a lot of new information every single day and we don´t actively repeat the lessons we have learned.

We have found a practical and 'stoic' solution for you.

This book is full of quotes from the ancient stoics and from modern day business people. A quote is the ideal medium, to deliver an important story or message in very compact way. **Only messages that get repeated will make it to our long-term memory.**

So my advice is to print the quotes used in ´Stoicism for Entrepreneurs´. Tape these quotes on your computer screen or on the bathroom mirror. A great way for a daily reminder for your personal road to more success and to hit the next level in your business.

If you want to be a productive entrepreneur:

- Go to:
  http://stoicismforentrepreneurs.businessleadershipplatform.com/

or

- Get the quotes
- print the quotes
- start reading

Enjoy the book.

Joel E. Winston

Table of Contents

Introduction	**9**
Who Were the Great Stoics?	12
A Brief Summary of Stoicism and Its Values	22
Chapter Summaries	28
Who Should Read This Book	32
How to Use this Book	34
Chapter 1: Stoicism and Journaling: Plan, Reflect and Achieve Success	**37**
Practical Advice and Tips for the Stoic Entrepreneur	50
Summary: The Chapter In Brief	60
Chapter 2: "Stoic, Prepare for the Worst!" Negative Visualization and the Secret to Overcoming Obstacles, Adversity and Failures	**61**
What is negative visualization and why is it beneficial?	64
Practical Advice and Tips for the Stoic Entrepreneur	67
Summary: The Chapter In Brief	78
Chapter 3: Get to Work, Stoic. How to use Stoicism to Increase Motivation, Cultivate Discipline, and Enhance Productivity	**81**
Tips for Increasing Motivation	82
Tips for Cultivating Stoic Discipline	84
Tips for Enhancing Productivity	85
The Importance of Taking Responsibility for the Outcome	87
How to Persevere In Spite of the Odds	88
Practical Advice and Tips for the Stoic Entrepreneur	90
Summary: The Chapter In Brief	91

Chapter 4: The Stoic in the World: How to Stoicism Can Improve Self-Confidence, Communication with Others and Make You a Better Negotiator — **93**

- Building Self-Confidence and Self-Awareness (introspection) — 94
- The Benefits of an Awareness of Others (extrospection) — 96
- How to Deal with Anger and Disappointment — 98
- Stoic Negotiation Tactics — 101
- Practical Advice and Tips for the Stoic Entrepreneur — 103
- Summary: The Chapter In Brief — 107

Chapter 5: Practical Examples of how Interconnectedness can help you relate to employees, partners, clients and improve your well being — **109**

- How to Deal with Poor Performance in Employees — 110
- How to Improve Relationships with Business Partners — 115
- Negotiation and Selling — 117
- How to Improve Your Relationship with Your Clients — 118
- How Stoicism Can Foster Optimal Wellness: — 120
- Practical Advice and Tips for the Stoic Entrepreneur — 125
- Summary: The Chapter In Brief — 134

Chapter 6: Conclusion: What the Stoics Can Teach Us about Obtaining and Maintaining Success in Business — **137**

Further Reading — **145**

Introduction

"First say to yourself what you would be, and then do what you have to do."

-Epictetus

What do you think of when you hear the word "stoic?" Do you imagine a person – maybe a half-crumbling marble statue in a museum that represents a towering Greek man – with a serious face, unflinching eyes, and a silent demeanor? Do you imagine a man who never shows his emotion, even in the toughest of circumstances?

Sure, today the commonplace usage of the word implies all that; in fact, the dictionary defines stoicism as "the endurance of pain or hardship without the display of feelings and without complaint." This might be the way you are used to hearing the word "stoic." But did you know that the word "stoic" actually belongs to a long philosophical tradition that began in ancient Greece, spread to Rome and then to the rest of the Western world?

Now, wait, before you start to yawn, stop for a second. This is not a philosophy that is meant for long hours of study and endless, fruitless pontification. To learn about stoicism you will not feel like you are back in your high school or college philosophy class, so do not worry. This is a philosophy that is all about taking action. It is about taking control of your emotions and obtaining self-mastery. And, most importantly, it is about getting things done.

To just give you a quick taste, think about these words of one famous stoic, Epictetus, with which this introduction began: "First say to yourself what you would be, and then do what you have to do." As these words suggest, this is a practical, concrete, no-nonsense, actionable philosophy that—if applied correctly—can help you in your daily life, as a person, and as a successful, busy entrepreneur. And, above all, it can help you decide what you would be and then do what you have to do, which is the secret to building the business of your dreams.

The philosophy known as stoicism all started on a porch of a man named Zeno in Athens, Greece, thousands of years ago. Today, some of the most powerful, wealthy businessmen in our country have been associated with stoicism. Men like

Apple visionary Steve Jobs, Microsoft creator Bill Gates, investment expert Warren Buffet, inventor extraordinaire Elon Musk, finance guru Tony Robbins, and start-up mogul Tim Ferris have been described as stoics. So, too, have Presidents from George Washington to Theodore Roosevelt and Barack Obama. Maybe it sounds surprising, but the world's toughest man, David Goggins, a former Navy Seal, and an ultramarathoner, also practice stoicism.

Do you wonder why some of the wealthiest people on the planet have turned to stoicism to help themselves do great, seemingly impossible things? Do you want to know how you can take advantage of this concrete, practical philosophic tradition to improve your business?

Using quotations and anecdotes from ancient Stoics—and advice from their modern-day counterparts—this book will guide you through the practical applications of stoicism and how they can help you become the best possible entrepreneur.

In this brief introduction, we will start by telling you about the five most famous stoics: Zeno of Citium considered the founder of stoicism. Then we will discuss his major followers:

Epictetus, Cato, Seneca and Marcus Aurelius. In a quick biographical sketch, we will tell you the major contributions they made to Stoic philosophy. Then, we will jump into an overview of what stoicism really believes, and after that, we will get started with our practical advice on how to harness the power of stoicism to improve your business, no matter what stage it is currently at. The historian Paul Veyne, a great admirer of Stoicism and an expert on ancient Rome, described Stoicism in this way: *"Stoicism is not so much an ethic as it is a paradoxical recipe for happiness."* If this sounds enticing, keep on reading!

Who Were the Great Stoics?

Zeno of Citium lived between 334 B.C. and 262 B.C. He was a Greek philosopher and is considered the founder of the Stoic school of thought. Zeno of Citium forms a bridge between stoicism and an earlier philosophic trend, the Cynic tradition (a philosophy that espouses a total rejection of society – which is connected to our current English, negative definition of the word).

Zeno of Citium was born on the island of Cyprus, off the coast of what is today known as of Turkey. He was the son of a merchant. He worked for his father for most of his life, until he founded the Stoic school of philosophy in Athens. At first, his students were referred to as Zenoans. However, he taught his lessons on a porch, and since the Greek word for the porch is "stoa," the lessons he taught became known as stoicism.

Zeno's original adherence to Cynicism influenced the development of Stoic philosophy. In Athens, before starting his own school, he studied with Crates of Thebes, the most famous Cynic philosopher of the time. Thanks to the influence of Crates of Thebes, Zeo lived a minimalist, even ascetic way of life, a quality you will see being extolled by modern practitioners of Stoicism like Tim Ferris and Warren Buffet. This Cynic influence carried over into his Stoic philosophy. He also adopted the Cynics' rhetorical speaking style, which was very blunt and direct. He engaged in scandalous behavior by spending his time with the lowest classes of society and making fun of the privileged elites. This contributed to making Stoicism seem accessible, which ensured its transmission through the centuries.

Zeno's belief in Stoicism shared some views with the Cynics. Both philosophies believed in a single, virtuous good that is the only goal a moral person should try to pursue. One of his most important teachings is that "Man conquers the world by conquering himself." He taught that having a lack of passion ("apatheia" – apathy) is essential. If a person can control his desires and his emotions, this will allow him to gain wisdom and be able to apply that wisdom to everyday life. In order to achieve this state, Zeno advocated the cultivation of indifference—to pleasure and to pain—possibly with the help of regular meditation practice.

Another important stoic idea that comes from Zeno is the idea that all living beings should behave according to the laws of nature. This idea, known as "kathekon," has been translated as "proper function" or "appropriate behavior for nature" or "befitting actions." This should be the Stoic's ultimate objective. Finally, Zeno is also responsible for the Stoics' acceptance of destiny, which some have criticized as being a form of extreme resignation or pessimism. However, as we will discuss, this pessimism actually has a major benefit and, in fact, is more powerful than optimism.

When he died, Zeno was a loved and respected philosopher. Thanks to the influence he spread amongst the people of his time, a tomb was built in his honor, and his stoic teachings continued on through his pupil Cleanthes of Assos. Today, we do not have any of Zeno's writings, although we believe he wrote a book, *Republic,* that was written as an imitation or a critique of Plato's famous work. All of his quotations and anecdotes survive thanks to a large number of followers, such as Epictetus (see below) who wrote about him in their own works. Few people know this, but another philosopher from the time, Chrysippus, is actually credited with developing most of the philosophical doctrines that are currently understood as stoicism.

The next important stoic who will play a major role in this book is **Epictetus**. Epictetus was born in about 55 C.E. in what is today south-western Turkey. He was sold into slavery as a boy and grew up in Rome. His owner was Epaphroditus, who had himself once been a slave of the famous Emperor Nero. Epictetus was able to study stoicism—which had been developing for more than four hundred years since the establishment of Zeno's popular school in Athens. The afflictions he suffered as a slave left him physically impaired, but that only strengthened his commitment to studying and living philosophy. Thanks to this experience as a slave, Epictetus inspired people of all different class backgrounds, including the most disadvantaged, to adhere to Stoicism as a possible way of gaining emotional freedom in difficult circumstances.

After gaining his freedom, Epictetus went to Greece where he founded his own school of Stoic teaching. He believed that a Stoic teacher had the duty to help his students live the philosophy, which would lead to a life led "according to nature." He also believed in the importance of *apatheia* like Zeno.

President Theodore Roosevelt was known to carry copies of Epictetus' writings with him while he undertook his incredible journeys, like his exploration of the most dangerous rivers of the South American Amazon. Decorated United States' Admiral James Stockdale attributes his ability to survive as a POW in Vietnam to Epictetus' wisdom and teachings.

Next, we introduce you to **Cato** (the younger) who was born in 95 BC in Rome and died in 46 BC. His parents died when he was young, and he grew up surrounded by tragedy (his uncle was assassinated when he was only four years old). As a statesman in the late Roman Republic, he constantly used his speech-giving skills to preach values of tenacity and integrity.

Cato was famous for resisting bribes and rejecting the flourishing corruption of the times in which he lived.

Thanks to his unflappable moral standards, Cato captured the imagination of many artists and writers, including the medieval writer, Dante, who placed him in a prestigious spot in his epic *Divine Comedy*. Later, in the 18th century, Joseph Addison wrote a play called *Cato: A Tragedy* that helped preserve the Stoic legacy. General George Washington so admired Cato that he staged a performance of Addison's tragedy during the Revolutionary War in order to inspire the troops and improve their sagging morale.

Cato was beloved by public servants like Washington, as well as the other founding fathers who carefully read and studied his works; President John Adams was also a great admirer. The founding fathers saw him as a symbol of liberty that inspired them while they fought for freedom from Great Britain's more powerful empire. President Barack Obama has also been compared to Cato; President Bill Clinton once described Obama as "a man cool on the outside, but who burns for America on the inside."

Cato never wrote an autobiography, so his teachings are less known today than the other Stoics. However, he left three important lessons that we will discuss more fully throughout the book: that we should learn from pain, insist on uncompromisingly high standards, and keep fear in its proper place.

The next Stoic who made a major influence on the philosophy is **Seneca,** a Stoic associated with the Roman Empire. Seneca lived from 1 B.C.E to 65 C.E. He was born in Cordoba, Spain, but lived his life in Rome, where he studied rhetoric and philosophy. He was known as a successful politician and dramatic person. In many of his writings, he reflects on the danger of ambition and the power of emotion—topics about which he knew a lot, thanks to his powerful role in the Roman empire. (He was an adviser to Emperor Nero). Because he came much later in the Stoic tradition, Seneca is better known for expounding on and passing down Stoic ideas and teachings, rather than creating his own new terminology.

Seneca wrote in Latin and his works have been central in preserving the understanding of Stoicism in the modern era. In fact, in the Renaissance, his works were discovered by philosophers and artists and influenced their work at that time as well.

Finally, we come to **Marcus Aurelius.** Known as "the Philosopher," Marcus Aurelius was a Roman emperor from 161 AD to 180 AD. The last of the "five good emperors" who presided over the end of the empire's peaceful era (Pax Romana), Aurelius was also the author of *Meditations,* a collection of personal philosophical writings that are the most significant basis for our present-day understanding of stoicism. In *Meditations,* he discusses the influence of earlier Stoics, such as Epictetus; but scholars believe he most likely had never gotten to read works by other stoic forefathers such as Seneca. It was thanks to his stoical framework that he was able to acquire the necessary self-mastery that enabled him to thrive in the unbearably challenging role of emperor of the world's most powerful empire. Former President Bill Clinton is said to read *Meditations* every year, and James Mattis, Secretary of Defense, took the book with him when serving abroad in the military. Even the former Prime Minister of China, Wen Jiabao, is a devoted reader of Marcus Aurelius.

Beyond the original teachers, stoicism is and has been embraced by world leaders, from kings and presidents to cultural figures to entrepreneurs. At seventeen, George Washington was introduced to Stoicism and talked to his men about Cato during the Revolutionary War. Thomas Jefferson is said to have had a copy of Seneca on his nightstand when he died. Great economists, like Adam Smith, were stoics, and the political genius John Stuart Mill, celebrated stoicism as "the highest ethical product of the ancient mind." Even President Barack Obama has been described as a stoic.

Stoicism also inspired contemporary psychotherapy, known as cognitive behavior therapy or CBT. CBT openly credits stoic philosophers for its values and practices. The quotation of Epictetus' "It's not the events that upset us, but our judgments about the events," was an early mantra taught to CBT patients. Many famous psychotherapists, such as Paul DuBois, have assigned patients homework from classical stoic texts as part of their treatment.

The fact that stoicism has not only survived but *thrived* for thousands of years, and that so many world leaders and mental health professionals have embraced its principles, speaks volumes to its tremendous power. Most likely that power derives from the fact that Stoicism is not a religion (although people have described it as a religion for the non-religious). Instead, it is a living, breathing set of practices that were developed according to the people who practiced it, in order to meet their changing needs. This means that it is a philosophy still being generated and, thus, in order to survive, needs our new contributions. In order to make sure it does not fall out of view, we must adapt it to our present moment, to ensure it remains useful and usable. After all, the core principles of Stoicism are too valuable for us to allow them to fade away. This means that as soon as you begin practicing Stoicism, you are also free to adapt it to suit your needs. (Just make sure you first learn the principles carefully!)

In the next section, we will discuss briefly each of the main ideas of stoicism—a philosophy that is committed to the idea of *practice*. It is not a dry, dead philosophy that you'd find in a dusty book written by someone who never lived outside of a university library. Think of it more like the warm-up for your workout in the gym or an intense yoga class. It is made to be practiced hand-in-hand with your life and work, to help you live the best possible life.

A Brief Summary of Stoicism and Its Values

Stripped down to its most basic essential components, we can say that the Stoic person aims to find the truth and to do what is right. However, of course, Stoicism is more complex than that. Although Stoic *ethics* is the most famous branch of stoic philosophy (that we will be focusing on here), stoicism is actually made up of three branches of study: ethics, physics and logic.

This helps us to remember that Stoics were not abstract thinkers but, in fact, studied the entire world around them. So, just to briefly mention the other two branches: Physics refers to the s study of natural science or metaphysics. Logic refers to rhetoric and knowledge, which today would translate into psychology and social sciences, as well as public speaking and communication.

The philosophy of stoicism is focused on the pursuit of virtue, which stoics believe is the true source of happiness, instead of the acquisition of material wealth, power or human attachment. But what is truly good? How do we know what we are supposed to pursue? The first group of things to value according to the Stoics is: temperance (i.e. self-control), justice, courage and wisdom. These personal or spiritual qualities that are part of one's character are referred to as virtues. The second group of things to value include wealth, beauty and personal gifts (such as strength, good vision, hearing or eyesight, intelligence, etc.), good birth (this concept is slightly outdated today, although no one can deny the benefits of being well connected), power and honors. Socrates, one of the earliest and greatest Greek thinkers who influenced the Stoics, believed that for these things to actually be of any real benefit, they must be used properly, and with wisdom. This means that for the second group of goods to be truly *good*, a person must also have the first group of goods. This is because the virtues are what guide our actions. And what are virtues for? They are the qualities that allow us to choose the things that are right for us and to act in such a way that we always pursue the good option.

For the Stoics, the most important thing a person can do in his life is to improve his character in accordance with virtue. This means that he must behave with extreme self-control, act with justice towards all of his fellow men, and be courageous in his decisions and his behaviors. This kind of behavior will, according to the Stoics, result in a good and happy life.

The words of Epictetus elegantly speak to this understanding of philosophy. He writes, "Philosophy does not promise to secure anything external for man, otherwise it would be admitting something that lies beyond its proper subject-matter. For as the material of the carpenter is wood, and that of statuary bronze, so the subject-matter of the art of living is each person's own life." Seneca also had words of wisdom in this regard, claiming that self-knowledge is the most valuable knowledge of all. He writes, "believe me, it is better to have knowledge of the ledger of one's own life than of the corn-market." This is particularly apt saying for someone who is interested in becoming (or perhaps already is) a successful entrepreneur. In our culture, we often value people for how much knowledge they possess about *things*—especially where the money is concerned. However, the Stoics tell us to keep in mind that our own life has a ledger—a balance book—and this is the hardest and most valuable thing to master.

Because of this emphasis on philosophy's power to transform a person, Stoicism is the ideal belief system for someone interested in self-improvements, like a current or aspiring business owner or entrepreneur. Stoicism is a simple but profound set of beliefs, and it is made up of a series of sayings, guidelines and exercises that anyone can follow as part of their daily routine. The daily routine actually becomes a part of the stoic way of life, not just an accessory, as we will discuss.

So if these principles apply to improve our individual behavior, what does Stoicism have to say about the world around us? Stoicism acknowledges the uncertainty and precarity of human existence. The Stoics believe that we cannot control events outside of ourselves and thus, cannot rely on them for happiness. Included in this definition are our physical bodies, for although we can do our best to take care of ourselves, eat well, get exercise, and seek medical treatment, we can only go so far with that—as any person who has ever lost a loved one to an illness knows. Furthermore, we do not decide how we look or what strengths or weaknesses we might have, or even if we are born able-bodied or disabled. All we can count on is our minds and how it reacts to the chaotic world around us—and within us. As Epictetus observes: "For good or for ill, life and nature are governed by laws that we can't change. The quicker we accept this, the more tranquil we can be. Freedom comes from understanding the limits of our power and the natural limits set in place by divine providence. By accepting life's limits and inevitabilities and working with them rather than fighting them, we become free." So the Stoics encourage you to recognize who you are. This means understanding both what you are great at and what you struggle with. Then, you can make the most of your gifts and learn to work with—not against—your natural limitations.

Beyond our individual selves, the Stoics remind us that we are part of a larger family and society. This means that every choice we make will have repercussions on other people, whether we know it or not. No one can possibly be self-sufficient. This interdependence is celebrated by the Stoics because a network of cooperation helps forge strong communities, which is the bedrock of human culture—the foundation on which great societies are built. However, this interrelatedness also creates the biggest challenges, because it requires that people learn to separate what is in their control from what is in the control of others. Stoicism, therefore, is very focused on giving instructions for how to deal with these inevitable, complicated and vital interactions.

Stoicism does have a few core beliefs that are easy to understand and to follow. One of its central principles is to remember how very short our life is. Seneca described this truth in this way: "It is not that we have so little time but that we lose so much. ... The life we receive is not short but we make it so; we are not ill provided but use what we have wastefully." Apple CEO Steve Jobs famously reflected on this principle, telling people, "If you live each day as it was your last, someday you'll most certainly be right."

If death is one of the few certainties of life, everything else in the world is unpredictable. In the face of the uncertainty of life, stoicism tells us to be strong and self-controlled. The Greek word for self-control is, *sophrosune,* which sounds completely foreign to us, but the Latin, *temperentia* sounds just like the old-fashioned English term "temperance." Today we might translate it as "moderation," but the important thing to remember is that all these terms have the same implication: a disposition towards controlling a person's most intense desires and when he feels those desires, to do so in a more controlled and moderate way. One of the key terms of stoicism is the concept of self-mastery, not to avoid emotions but to control them. (This is why the dictionary definition of stoicism, cited above, refers to the lack of visible emotions.) So why do we need moderation? As stoicism warns us, the reason for most people's unhappiness is that they constantly rely on their emotions and their senses, when they should only be depending on clear logic and reason.

Most importantly for us here, Stoicism doesn't concern itself with complicated hypotheses about the world, but with helping us overcome destructive emotions and act on what can be acted upon. It is built for action, not endless, fruitless debate. The Stoics focus on the banal, every day and the mundane issues every person faces. Therefore, stoicism, as a philosophy, enables us to become stronger, by recognizing that all people—ourselves included!—are imperfect. Stoicism does not need a university degree in Philosophy to be comprehended. It does not even require extensive study, research, writing, and discussion. However, it will not be enough to just quote the Stoics to look good at parties or download Stoic apps on your cellphone. It simply needs to be lived, practiced and experienced. Epictetus summarized this stoic belief in the following quotation, that will be an excellent conclusion for this chapter: "Don't explain your philosophy. Embody it."

Chapter Summaries

In the chapters that follow, we will take you through the main teachings of Stoicism, using the Stoics words as a guide. Each chapter will focus on a different topic, with activities and practices geared towards helping you as an entrepreneur improve your life from a Stoic perspective. We will also incorporate advice from contemporary successful Stoics, that can guide you towards achieving your business goals.

Chapter 2: Stoicism and Journaling: Plan, Reflect and Achieve Success

Chapter two introduces you to the essential Stoic practice of daily journaling. As Seneca once said, "A person who is not aware that he is doing anything wrong has no desire to be put right. You have to catch yourself doing it before you can reform." Chapter two explains why morning and evening reflections together make the perfect bookend to a stoic day and give you advice about how to start your own journal to achieve a clear vision and to glean important lessons from what you have done. The Journal reminds us of the importance of daily improvement and gives us a clean slate every single day, encouraging us to live in the present as the stoics encouraged.

Chapter 3: "Stoic, Prepare for the Worst!" Negative Visualization and the Secret to Overcoming Obstacles, Adversity and Failures

Negative visualization is a pillar of stoic philosophy. By mentally confronting our worst fears through the development of a mental training ground, we can immunize ourselves against them. Beyond the mental comfort, negative visualization also prepares us for the "worst-case scenario" and encourages us to have a safety net for whatever life might bring. This chapter will explain why for the businessman, this is essential.

Chapter 4: Get to Work, Stoic. How to use Stoicism to Increase Motivation, Cultivate Discipline, and Enhance Productivity

Chapter 4 is the most stoic of all the chapters because it is all about action. This chapter gets into the nitty-gritty about how you can to increase your motivation, cultivate the strongest possible discipline and optimize your productivity by delegating, automating and letting go. It ends by giving tips about what a stoic leader should do after: take ownership of any results, good or bad, and persevere through any challenges—which is what actually makes us stronger than our successes. As Epictetus once said, "Give yourself fully to your endeavors. Decide to construct your character through excellent actions and determine to pay the price of a worthy goal. The trials you encounter will introduce you to your strengths."

Chapter 5: The Stoic in the World: How to Stoicism Can Improve Self-Confidence, Communication with Others and Make You a Better Negotiator

Chapter 5 discusses how introspection and extrospection work to put you in the strongest possible position as an entrepreneur. By knowing yourself and others, as used in Stoic philosophy, you can bring the knowledge together for the benefit of your business. After all, knowing yourself is key to one of the foundational business skills: negotiating.

Chapter 6: Practical Examples about How a sense of interconnectedness can help you relate to employees, partners, clients and improve your well being

Introducing the concept of *sympatheia* or interconnectedness, chapter 6 offers advice about how to make the most of your relationships with employees, business partners, and clients. What do you do when an employee performs poorly? How do you react when a business partner criticizes you? How do you win and keep clients? After giving you advice from the Stoic perspective, the chapter also takes a deeper look at negotiation and selling tactics for the stoic entrepreneur. The chapter then concludes with actionable advice about your individual wellbeing. As we will discuss, stoicism can actually show you how to conserve precious energy, decrease damaging stress, and sharpen your time management skills. This chapter contains **a series of exercises, including a stoic week that you can use to lead your employees through at work.**

Chapter 7: Conclusion: What The Stoics Can Teach Us about Obtaining and Maintaining Success in Business

Finally, chapter 7 will wrap everything up and provide a quick, handy summary of everything that we have discussed throughout the entire book, so feel free to use it as a reference guide while you are working through the application of each of the different principles.

Who Should Read This Book

Now that we've introduced you to the major stoics and what they believed, we hope you are starting to get the feeling that stoicism is for you. But just in case you still have any doubts, let's talk briefly about who should read this book. In a word, anyone who considers themselves an entrepreneur—or who hopes, someday, to become one. Obviously, entrepreneurs are a naturally diverse group of individuals. An entrepreneur could be a CEO of a major corporation or a creative developer inside of an established one. An entrepreneur could be a visionary who is planning a start-up, or it could be a self-employed freelancer who is hoping to grow her business. They are always thinking about how to improve themselves and the world around them. And let's not forget, young people are sometimes the truest of entrepreneurs. A child selling lemonade at the side of the road with a handmade sign, or the middle school kid who turns his iPhone into a DJ setup to turn his friends' gathering into a party—and then markets himself to the rest of his school, is an entrepreneur.

Do any of these descriptions apply to you or the people you know? One thing all these different kinds of entrepreneurs have in common is that they are passionate people who are not content to accept the status quo. They like to think, and they think fast. Their thoughts are original, and they welcome change and novelty—but only insofar as it advances their chosen, deeply held beliefs. Even if this doesn't quite apply to you yet, do you wish that it did? Stoicism will teach you to embrace these values and to shed the misguided values that are not serving you in your entrepreneurial journey. Because stoics recognize the world for what it is—uncertain, ever-changing and full of valuable lessons—they make the ideal businessmen: guided by ideals but grounded in reality.

So whether you're an entrepreneur within a company, are already running a company and want to break through to the next level, are self-employed and hoping to expand, or are just nursing the smallest seed of a startup idea, turn to an ancient, time-tested philosophical practice and see what results come to you.

How to Use this Book

With so many different kinds of readers, we recognize that everyone will interact with this book as he or she needs. But here is some guidance as to how we envision our reader's journey so that you can decide how to make the most of it. First, let us say that you should feel free to read this book cover-to-cover. Also, each chapter is contained within itself, so if you see a topic that grabs your interest, feel free to read them in any order you choose. However, even if you do read it all at once the first time, in order to get the best results from this book, we recommend that you go back and read it again slowly a second time, if not more. Focus closely on one chapter every week or even every month. Use the "Practical Advice and Tips for the Stoic Entrepreneur" section to form new habits, picking one at a time until it is fully internalized for at least one week (or even more). Only then when you are confident that you have mastered all the activities and principles should you then move on to the next chapter.

We believe that if you carefully follow all the "Practical Advice and Tips for the Stoic Entrepreneur," and apply them methodically to your daily life, you will see incredible, measurable results in your business, no matter what your background is and no matter what your goals are. Stoicism can help you as an entrepreneur whether you are a business of one or the head of a large organization, and whether you are in the planning phases or a seasoned executive looking for a new direction. So let's stop the introducing and go get started!

Chapter 1: Stoicism and Journaling: Plan, Reflect and Achieve Success

"When you arise in the morning, think of what a privilege it is to be alive, to think, to enjoy, to love." –Marcus Aurelius

For the Stoic philosophy, the single twenty-four-hour day is the most important unit of time. This becomes clear when we reflect on what Seneca once wrote, "Begin at once to live, and count each separate day as a separate life." This appreciation for a single day means that practicing the stoic way of life must begin the moment you open your eyes before your feet even touch the floor. After all, Seneca tells us, "As each day arises, welcome it as the very best day of all, and make it your own possession. We must seize what flees."

When you first wake up in the morning, Marcus Aurelius urges people to reflect on their life with gratitude. He tells you to think about the simple, most basic elements of what it means to be a human: to think, to enjoy and to love. Acquiring an appreciative mindset, that is focused on the truly important things, will be key to fully embodying the stoic way of life and reaping the countless benefits. A good way to imagine your mind is as your personal, impenetrable fortress, inside which you can escape from the tumultuous, chaotic world around you. As Marcus Aurelius *writes,* "'Men seek retreats for themselves, houses in the country, sea-shores, and mountains... But this is altogether a mark of the most common sort of men, for it is in your power to choose to retire into yourself.'" This comes in handy during the busy day of an entrepreneur. You probably will be too busy to take a regular retreat at a beach house, but no one is too busy to start the day with some quiet, guided reflection.

So, start the morning with a feeling of gratitude for your life, within the fortress of your mind. However, it is not enough to just let these ideas pass through your mind as you go through your morning routine – it would be far too simple to get carried away into your regular habits, and forget all about the Stoics. If you want to truly become a Stoic, you need to find a way to make this morning reflection a habitual part of your existence that keeps its values front and center. For this reason, Stoics recommends taking up the habit of daily journaling.

Before we explain to you the *how* of Stoic journaling, we'll take a minute to reflect on why: for stoics, journaling is not just something to do. For Stoics, journalism *is* stoicism. The daily practice of mindful, written reflection is a central facet of stoicism. Sure, some of the stoics journals were published (like Marcus Aurelius' *Meditations*). Today, modern-day stoics like Tim Ferris also publish their writings online for millions of devoted followers. That's fine for them, and helpful for us, as we can benefit from their wisdom. However, you should not start this habit with an eye towards getting a fancy book deal, starting a viral blog, or even updating your social media and collecting as many "likes" as possible. Journaling should be for yourself. It should allow you to access your most private fears and thoughts and goals. Essentially, it should be a gateway that allows you to access the depths of your true self. This is impossible to achieve if you are constantly thinking about who your readers might be or how many clicks your post will get. Always remember: YOU are your most important reader. So write for yourself. After his experience with journaling, Seneca remarked, "I am beginning to be my own friend." Then, he reflected: someone who is able to be a friend to himself is able to be a friend to everyone around him. So do not think you are being selfish by keeping your self-reflections private; in fact, eventually, you might want to share them. But before you get to sharing, remember that by improving yourself you are becoming a better friend, father, boss, community member, etc., to those around you.

If you have never done it before, the next question that will come into your mind is: So how do you start a journal? In the "Practical Advice and Tips for the Stoic Entrepreneur" section below, we give you some challenges and exercises to try in order to commit to the daily practice. Here, we go over some other foundational details that will help you begin journaling in no time. And, more importantly, it will get you so committed to journaling that it will become an automatic habit both at the beginning and at the end of your day, every single day.

First things first: What kind of journal should you use, paper or electronic? The most important way to answer this question is to ask yourself, what kind of journal would I be most likely to use? Honestly, at the end of the day, all that matters is that you write. Do not waste hours searching for the *perfect* journal. You do not want that to become an unnecessary distraction. But if you want it, here's our advice:

We prefer a physical, paper journal. It could be a basic notebook without any special features at all. Many companies sell pre-printed goal journals that aim to get you to fill out every aspect of your life, including your daily schedule, all of your thoughts of gratitude, short and long-term goals, and more. They might even provide you with inspirational quotations. These companies often break up time into thirteen-week chunks (one quarter of a year). This matches up with Benjamin Franklin's famous virtue challenge, in which he strived for self-improvement by working on himself for thirteen weeks. (Although he claims he did not ultimately attain true perfection, Franklin remarked that he benefitted greatly from the act of journaling itself and—like a true stoic—he believed that going through the *process* was the really beneficial part, rather than obtaining his specific, lofty goal).

If you want to try a commercial goal journal, go ahead. If you are a beginner, they provide excellent structure, and the daily, weekly and monthly planning features are very much in alignment with Stoic principles. However, if you want to skip all the bells and whistles, a basic lined notebook is absolutely fine. In fact, the Stoics would probably be more impressed with your simplicity! A handwritten journal is great because the very act of physically writing words on the page has been proven to make important neurological connections in our brain: Scientists have shown that we remember better when we handwrite concepts, as opposed to when we type them. A handwritten journal will also help you avoid temptation if you are thinking about immediately sharing your raw journal notes online. At the very least, if you want to turn them into a blog one day, you'll have to type them up—and this will give you a chance to reflect on whether that is the best course of action (and edit as necessary!). The paper journal also provides a nice break from the world of screens, if your business requires you to spend a lot of time online, as is the case with most people's businesses today. Finally, a physical journal will help you stay focused, as it will not be sending out competing notifications that tell you to check your email.

Of course, you can also journal online. This has its own advantages and disadvantages. The major advantages are that you can access it anywhere (if you use an online program). Another huge advantage is that after you have written for a while, you can use the search function to look for any trends over time: what words keep coming up in your journal? Maybe you are repressing a deeply desired goal! Or avoiding fear. Are you constantly journaling about money as a source of anxiety? Is there an employee whose name keeps coming up who is constantly frustrating you? This repetition can give you data to analyze as you plan your next step. You can also use the word count tool to keep track of how much you are writing. Do you start the week with a flood of words and get stingy as the week goes on (or get maybe burnt out)? Or does it take you a few days to warm up to writing? Before you get too excited about the online journal, do not forget that the disadvantage is that you can easily become distracted by the rest of the internet. Once you have truly mastered the stoic principles, you will not have a problem for you to remain completely focused on the task at hand. But since you are still at the very beginning, if you want to journal online, consider turning off your wifi or putting blockers on sites or programs that tempt you. The online journal might also cause you to be tempted to turn your diary into a public document, which we do not recommend at this early stage in your stoic development.

So, whether you decide to use a beat-up old notebook or your fancy new laptop, what do you do once you start your journal? First, one thing is certain: you will not be successful if you do not have a clear objective in mind. As Seneca wrote, "If a person doesn't know to which port they sail, no wind is favorable." Therefore, when you start your journal for the day, you must start with a clear plan. A good way to approach this is to ask yourself: where do I want to be at the end of the day? How will I know I have been successful? What keywords do I want to use to shape my metaphorical travels today? If you are running a business, large or small, you obviously have countless things to do in one short day, which makes a plan even more important for you. Say you know you need to hire a new employee, upgrade your software, consult your accountant and meet with potential new clients. How do you use journaling to help yourself prioritize?

Start with five minutes of free writing. This means you should put down whatever comes to mind, without thinking about it too hard. Nothing is too trivial: what you ate for breakfast, what song you heard on the radio, think of these first sentences as "clearing your throat." Now tune in to what is around you. Is it noisy or quiet? What about your desk and your chair? Are you comfortable? Are you breathing regularly? Are you already looking around for your next cup of coffee? Do not judge yourself, just write it down. There will be plenty of time to make adjustments once you have gotten some data down.

Now, once you have started to let the ideas flow and are getting past the first few moments of throat clearing, ask yourself what issues are starting to come up to the foreground. Once you have gotten a clear handle on what is surfacing in your mind, you can start to figure out how that information can be used to help you with your day. Ask yourself: Are you unable to meet with potential new clients because you can't find the time, in between handling your taxes and technology and a hundred other competing things? Okay, so maybe you need to prioritize hiring one or more new employees to help you out. Then decide to center your day around that objective. At the same time, you can't let your taxes be forgotten. Plan yourself a few fifteen- or twenty-minute blocks of time to get done the absolute essentials—but only after you have dedicated some serious time on advancing your job search. (When you develop a more keen sense of your daily schedule, you will also start to realize what times of the day you do your more optimal work, such as early morning, and will be able to designate those times to the crucial, complex objectives, while keeping up with less intensive, creative work during the times when you might be less sharp, for instance, right after lunch or at the end of the day.)

Do not forget, your first job in the journal is to plan for one single day, but there will also be medium- and long term goals that you still want to achieve, so note those down and see what smaller steps you can take to advance them. If your day is already feeling crowded, you can commit to a time when you will be working on those goals later in the week—and then keep your promise to yourself! Remember, as another stoic, Publius Syrus, once said, "Would you have a great empire? Rule over yourself." So you have to start treating the promises you make to yourself as seriously as the promises you make to your employees or clients.

Remember, a stoic knows what he wants from his day. He has a clear destination, a set plan of attack and measurable goals. And, in case you do not feel like you are not ready yet to trust the principles of an ancient tradition to guide your modern-day business, just remember that psychologists have proven the benefits of the Stoic way of life. Making a specific psychological commitment to an activity, and developing a concrete game plan, actually increases the likelihood of its achievement.

So, once you have got your plan down on paper (or on the screen), then it becomes the time to execute it. Here, we can go by the wise words of Marcus Aurelius, that should be an inspiration to you as you live out your plan. He writes, "Every hour focus your mind attentively---on the performance of the task in hand, with dignity, human sympathy, benevolence and freedom, and leave aside all other thoughts. You will achieve this if you perform each action as if it were your last." The only other thought you should allow into your mind is the brief mental notes about what worked and what did not about your daily plan. Maybe you forgot to budget at lunchtime and ate at your desk, which made your work slower. Maybe you left your door open and a colleague came in to chat with you, and you did not tell them you were busy. Maybe you gave yourself way too much time for your taxes, and then you were left with a random block of time with no goal. Do not worry about it, for now just make a mental note. During this initial phase, you are collecting as much data as possible for the new experiment that is your stoic life and work. This necessarily takes time; it simply cannot happen overnight. However, do not worry, because it *will* happen with patient, thoughtful, consistent reflection. Remember, Epictetus, tells us, "Progress is not achieved by luck or accident, but by working on yourself daily."

Aside from reflecting on your schedule, you will also want to note how things are going for your business itself. Did you score a new client at your meeting? Awesome—make a note and move on. Did the client seem uninteresting? Okay—make a note and move on. Remember, one of the central stoic principles is to set goals but to detach yourself from the outcome. As Epictetus once said, "Some things are within our power, while others are not. Within our power are opinion, motivation, desire, aversion, and, in a word, whatever is of our own doing; not within our power are our body, our property, reputation, office, and, in a word, whatever is not of our own doing." We will be discussing control and the body later, but for now, just make notes about what you are experiencing. Maybe you forgot your lunch at home and just ate snack bars and then could not focus well. Okay. Maybe you were exhausted after the team meeting and needed an extra cup of coffee. Okay. That's your body today. Maybe you were late for the meeting because of a traffic accident. Okay. Maybe it's raining and you got your suit wet. Okay. Just keep yourself focused on yourself and what you can control.

With all your data from the day you just lived, you will be heading into your evening reflection with a rich stash of information available for you to analyze objectively. There is nothing more valuable than your own lived experience—and most importantly, it is *yours*. Why would you throw away a free resource? Making use of this knowledge is exactly what will set you apart from your competitors and make you a great business person.

So even if you are completely exhausted, do not just sit down in front of the television at the end of the day. Go and get out of your journal once again. (And if you *are* exhausted, that is all the more reason to reflect on your schedule and figure out how to improve it so you are *not* exhausted tomorrow!) If you have written in a physical journal, maybe try to use a different color pen to write with and make markings right on top of the morning reflection. Act as if you were a stern, objective teacher. Star the places where you met your goals and circle the ones where you fell short of your objectives. Do not be too hard on yourself for the things that are outside of your control or too celebratory either. Your only job is to be fair. Find the good, the bad and, most importantly, extract the lessons you learned: were you exhausted after your meeting? Maybe go to bed earlier. Were you late for the meeting because of an accident? Do not forget to budget extra travel time. Did it rain on your new suit? Plan to check the weather every morning and bring an umbrella or, even better, make sure to keep a spare one in your car and a fresh change of clothes in your office.

Remember, one of the principles of stoicism is *apatheia*. This might sound like the English word *apathy,* which in casual speech means to not care. Instead, for the Stoics, *apatheia* means not eliminating but mastering one's emotions so that they do not make you deviate from your chosen life path. Most importantly, it means reframing the events of the day in the most helpful, positive way possible. At the end of the day, you must remember there is nothing you can do to change what happened. You can only change what you do going forward. Reframe any negative events and remember, that if you learned from them, they are not failures or setbacks but important building blocks for the future. The only failure would be to keep doing the same thing that does not work. As expert investor Warren Buffett once said, "You know ... you keep doing the same things and you keep getting the same result over and over again." Even though failure is an inevitable part of human existence, we can make the conscious choice to learn from those failures, even the most humiliating. A bad day does not have to become a terrible week. Use your journal to wipe the slate clean and stop the domino effect of cascading negativity when one single thing goes completely wrong. Seneca teaches us, "a gem cannot be polished without friction, nor a man without trials." So take your trials, and use them to polish you and your business into the diamond they both are.

Practical Advice and Tips for the Stoic Entrepreneur

How to Handle the Temptations of Technology: Stoicism, Self-Mastery and Digital Technology

In today's hyper-connected, social media world, it is harder than ever to live with clear intentions. How can we hope to develop and to execute a plan while social media sites like Facebook and Instagram use cutting-edge psychological research to try to distract us for as long as possible? After all, their business depends on it! When we casually surf the web, clicking from link to link with no specific objective, even though we might find many dead-ends, our brain is wired to hold out for the eventual "pay off" (whatever interesting link or article we might be searching for). Worse than that, because humans are social animals, our brain has an urgent need to monitor the "vital" information of how our social group perceives us. Social media allows us to monitor how much our friends are thinking about us, and it also shows how much we are thinking about them. This creates a feedback loop that exploits a vulnerability in human psychology. This powerful loop can cause us to waste precious hours of our day—and over time, these hours add up to huge amounts of time that we have just given away to these corporate giants, padding their bottom line and hurting our personal and economic wellbeing.

Fortunately, stoicism gives us the wisdom to defeat this powerful potential addiction. First, by planning out our day and sticking faithfully to whatever we have planned, we can decide how much time social media gets from us. If you have designated to spend fifteen minutes, make it fifteen minutes, not sixteen. You get to decide. (And, of course, if your business requires you to use social media, then by all means, use it – just be mindful of the impact it might be having on you and make sure to take occasional breaks.) If your business does *not* require social media, one option is that you could quit cold turkey. This is the approach that is recommended by experts in habits and social media: to stop using it completely for thirty days, during which time you need to cultivate other habits and in-person relationships. Particularly, from a stoic perspective, we would recommend reading books of great people in history to inspire you, and spending time in nature, another habit that scientists have proved actually works to increase productivity by giving your brain time to decompress.

If going cold turkey sounds too drastic for you, and you want to try to maintain and moderate your social media presence, there are free tracker apps that can help you limit yourself if you have not achieved self-mastery yet. Better yet, use social media as a tiny reward to reinforce your good behavior, and give yourself whatever limited amount of time *after* you achieve a goal for the day.

The other reason why social media is a potential pitfall for the stoic is that stoicism teaches us to avoid thinking about and being conditioned by how other people perceive us. If you're going to walk the stoic walk, you're going to have to stop being so concerned with how many "likes" you get. Every time you leap to grab your phone to see how many "likes" your latest post got, think about the words of Seneca, who once said, "We should not, like sheep, follow the herd of creatures in front of us, making our way where others go, not where we ought to go." And ask yourself...*would he be collecting likes?*

If you need further convincing, consider the thoughts of Arianna Huffington, the founder of the Huffington Post and Thrive Global, who is also a practicing stoic. She carries around the following quotation from Marcus Aurelius wherever she goes and has another copy on her desk and on her nightstand: "People look for retreats for themselves, in the country, by the coast, or in the hills. There is nowhere that a person can find a more peaceful and trouble-free retreat than in his own mind...So constantly give yourself this retreat, and renew yourself." She believes that this quotation "perfectly illustrates the current moment—right now that first retreat he's talking about is mostly digital. That's how we get away from ourselves—by retreating into technology and social media. But the only way to find peace and thrive is to take breaks from the world and make time to regularly renew ourselves by reconnecting with ourselves."

If the issue of technology is a major challenge for you, consider writing the Marcus Aurelius or Seneca quotation on a post-it note and hanging it above your work area or even on your bathroom mirror. Or, better yet, make it the background of your phone, so that you are forced to see it every time you want to go to participate in herd behavior.

Stoic Journaling Exercises for Success

Journaling and morning reflection: Once you have set limits on your major distractions, now it is time to get to the hard work of scrutinizing your life. Use your journal to write about your personal experience (do not think too much about others or about world events in this exercise). Each day's entry will be like a deposit in the bank that will add up to a valuable amount of data to allow you to analyze, using the tools of stoicism. This constant reflection will allow you to improve your business in the present—and the future. (If you already keep a journal, great. Keep going. Just make sure to avoid tangential reflections on other people or the world for now – we will get to the issue of "extrospection," or reflecting on other people, in a future chapter.) So what should you be writing? Remember what we discussed above, and try to think about your life as the Stoics would: calmly and with detachment, and with an objective eye towards self-improvement. Your writing can be a place where you voice your concerns privately, but then you should also take care to intervene and remind yourself of your objectives of self-mastery.

Evening Reflection: the evening reflection goes hand in hand with the morning reflection. If you do not do one, the other one will not have the same power. Think of them as bookends of your day. The evening is the perfect time to look back and reflect on what you have done in order to learn from your mistakes and strategize for what comes next. As you review your day in your mind, ask yourself the following questions: did I follow each of my principles in word and in deed? Was I professional and compassionate with all the people who I encountered? How did I better myself today? How did I better my business, my community and the world? Have I fought my vices and cultivated my virtues? (As you do this, you will naturally want to plan your next day. That is no problem, once you have completed the first portion of the activity. Write some notes for yourself for tomorrow, to set your next morning reflection off on a great foot.) One of the most important elements to focus on, is to think about how you reacted to any negative events or setbacks. Did you let them derail you? Were you able to accept them and move on? Better yet, were you able to learn from them? This might not happen immediately, but it is important to be moving in that direction. We will talk about this issue more in future chapters.

Finally, at the end of every single day, do not forget to remind yourself to practice *apatheia*. This day is finished and now there is nothing you can now do to make it go any differently. Whether good or bad, accept everything that has happened, and reframe it so that it can become a valuable lesson for the next time.

Advanced challenge: Kevin Rose, a major player in Silicon Valley and an aficionado of Stoicism, tries to incorporate a daily practice of surrender into his routine. He writes, "One thing I practice daily is surrender. I try to surrender to the earth as everything unfolds around me, not judging it, but accepting things as they are. This, of course, is easier said than done. One of my favorite quotes is from philosopher Alan Watts: "To have faith is to trust yourself to the water. When you swim, you don't grab hold of the water, because if you do, you will sink and drown. Instead, you relax and float."

Long-term challenge: Write a journal entry every day for one month, weekends included. Read the morning entry every single evening, and make notes as needed to evaluate your strengths and weaknesses. In each entry, try to write down one area of your business you want to improve the next day, no matter how small. If you keep improving one tiny thing per day for months, you will be surprised at how your business changes.

At the end of the week and of the month, do a quick overview of the past seven or thirty days to be ready to move forward strong. Some contemporary Stoics recommend a yearly ritual as well to celebrate 365 days of commitment to self-improvement and to provide a powerful overview of how far you have come.

Remember, your journal can also be an excellent place for you to make notes on this book as you are reading and to collect the most significant Stoic quotations you find within its pages or out in the world beyond. You can also use it to create your own glossary of the new terms you are learning to make sure you are incorporating them into your world view.

Bonus challenge: Now might be a good time to read Marcus Aurelius' philosophical journal, *Meditations,* to see the original stoic journaler in action. Many of the most successful politicians and entrepreneurs today are regular readers of Marcus Aurelius. Try joining them and see what happens!

Maximizing your schedule: Use Where You have Been to Help You Shape Where You Are Going

The goal of this activity is not to cram in as much as you possibly can into every single minute of every single day. Instead, the aim is to achieve the ideal, optimized weekly schedule to allow yourself to be as productive as possible in the long term. (Remember, it's a marathon, not a sprint!) First, however, in order to do this, you need data. After you have spent one week doing your morning and evening journaling, look back over all of your notes. Ask yourself: When do you work? Are you checking your phone? How long is each of your meal breaks? Are you getting any exercise, preferably outdoors and with friends? Do you remember to drink plenty of water? If you do not have enough information about all these components of your schedule, consider taking an entire week in which you write down everything you do. Be super detailed in your analysis. This will give you a baseline to increase productivity. Then, build an ideal schedule, with everything divided into fifteen- to thirty-minute blocks. When you work, only focus on that single thing. There are free online time trackers that can be useful in keeping detailed notes about what you do, especially because you can use them to identify problematic trends by searching across days, weeks or months.

Remember: Schedule in meals, rest, and outdoor activity. Even schedule in time to talk to your friends, have quality time with your family and go on social media if that is important to you. Make sure and actually relax during those times. The mind is like a muscle that, if well treated, can be primed to perform at the highest levels. Or if it is overworked, on the contrary, it can easily fall prey to injury, which ends up costing you in the long run. Do not forget, as Seneca said: "We must indulge the mind and from time to time allow it the leisure which is its food and strength. We must go for walks out of doors so that the mind can be strengthened by a clear sky and plenty of fresh air." In order to prepare yourself for the greatest daily challenges facing an entrepreneur, you will need to make sure your mind is in top form.

One small parenthesis here: there is a debate in contemporary Stoic communities about whether or not the Stoic should actually seek to optimize his or her environment, in order to make life easier. On the one hand, they argue that it is necessary to eliminate distractions in order to get to the things in life that matter. On the other hand, some argue that a true Stoic would not make things easy and should struggle through all the challenges of his outside world. (After all, he will not be able to control them all indefinitely, so he should learn how to do so.) Greg Sadler of modernstoicism.com weighs the evidence for each of these points and he ultimately concludes that because it is truly difficult to become a Sage (a fully realized Stoic), in the meantime, people should do what is best in terms of making a conducive environment for Stoic productivity. The important thing is that they recognize that it is only possible to control so much: a person can budget a perfect hour of creative work, and then the internet might crash, or the gardeners might start mowing right outside his or her window. But if you can make it easier for yourself, especially in these early stages, do it. There will be plenty of other areas you can use to develop and test your Stoic mettle, as we will discuss in future chapters.

Now that we have worked towards crafting our ideal day, week and month, and we know how to use it to optimize our time and constantly learn from ourselves, in the next chapter we will turn to one of the most challenging and rewarding parts of stoicism: the way we should handle the future. We will discuss the benefits of the "worst-case scenario" thinking, to make sure you anticipate any potential failures well ahead of time. This will allow you to put a security plan into place and master any lingering anxiety you have about taking necessary bold action.

Summary: The Chapter In Brief

Chapter two takes on the Stoic practice of journaling. Journaling is not just something that stoics do, it actually *is* stoicism. Morning and evening reflections together make the perfect bookend to a stoic day. It forces you to start every single morning with a clear vision of what you want to achieve. It makes you put your objectives foremost in your mind and push everything else to the side. Then, at the end of the day, it gives you a valuable perspective that derives from whatever lessons you happened to have learned, whether they are good or bad. And the best news? No matter what happened during one day, the next day, you have the privilege of waking up with a clean slate and starting the process over again—and again. And again. When you have done your journaling for a few weeks, do not forget to look back and spend a week optimizing your schedule. That way, you can identify productive and unproductive patterns, do your most important work at the time of day during which you are most creative, and make sure you are giving yourself the necessary rest to achieve your fullest potential.

Chapter 2: "Stoic, Prepare for the Worst!" Negative Visualization and the Secret to Overcoming Obstacles, Adversity and Failures

"When you are going to perform an act, remind yourself what kind of things the act may involve. When going to the swimming pool, reflect on what may happen at the pool: some will splash the water, some will push against one another, others will abuse one another, and others will steal. Thusly you have mentally prepared yourself to undertake the act, and you can say to yourself: I now intend to bathe, and am prepared to maintain my will in a virtuous manner, having warned myself of what may occur. Do this for every act, so that if any hindrance does emerge, you can think: I did not prepare myself only to undertake the act, but also for this hindrance that has occurred, and also to handle this hindrance virtuously and keep my will conformed to nature — and this will be impossible if I become vexed."

-Epictetus

All across any social media site today, you will see a culture of optimism popping up everywhere you look. Instagram gurus will tell you to think positively so that you can attract only the best energy into your life and work. Optimism is such a popular trend, and of course, the people who practice it claim to be happy (because that is the whole point, after all!). However, we should ask ourselves: is it *really* the ideal mindset for preparing you for success? The Stoics would say, "no." If you want to know how to prepare for and deal with, the obstacles, adversity, and failures that will inevitably come with being a successful entrepreneur, you will need to master the technique of negative visualization and understand why it can help.

Consider this quotation from Epictetus, as he prepares himself for the simple act of going swimming in a pool (do not worry, we will talk about more challenging, business-related activities later). As he does this, he goes through in his mind all the different negative things that people might do to him while he is there: he starts with small things, like getting splashed, then moves to medium things like getting jostled by someone, and finally he considers truly rotten things like facing abuse or theft. Running through this potential catalog of bad experiences does not make Epictetus anxious. In fact, it helps prepare him to make the most of his swim. By preparing himself to go swimming and making a mental contingency plan for any negative outcomes, he feels most ready to maintain his composure, thus allowing him to respond in accordance with his principles (i.e. virtuously).

In this exercise, Epictetus is thinking about all the possible things that *others* might do to him, that is the things that are outside of his control. Making this distinction is crucial for the stoic philosophy. He once wrote, "The chief task in life is simply this: to identify and separate matters so that I can say clearly to myself which are externals under my control, and which have to do with the choices I actually control." In the swimming pool, he cannot decide who splashes him, who pushes him, who abuses him and who steals from him. What he can do, is decide how *he* acts in response: he can choose to keep his calm composure, to maintain his virtue and to respond accordingly. After all, Epictetus reminds us, "We cannot choose our external circumstances, but we can always choose how we respond to them."

The key to successfully enacting this plan is to keep your rational mind in charge of your emotions. This allows you to stay completely calm and self-controlled. The negative visualization is exactly the Stoic tool that makes this possible. As Marcus Aurelius explained, "The first rule is to keep an untroubled spirit. The second is to look things in the face and know them for what they are." The Stoics use negative visualization in order to cultivate an ability to scrutinize a situation and understand every single aspect of it before they spring into action.

What is negative visualization and why is it beneficial?

> "What is quite unlooked for is more crushing in its effect, and unexpectedness adds to the weight of a disaster. The fact that it was unforeseen has never failed to intensify a person's grief. This is a reason for ensuring that nothing ever takes us by surprise. We should project our thoughts ahead of us at every turn and have in mind every possible eventuality instead of only the usual course of events."
> -Seneca

Have you ever witnessed up close the response of a person who experienced a terrible tragedy? Maybe a wife betrayed by her husband for decades. A businessman cheated by his longtime partner. An athlete sidelined by an unexpected injury. Have you ever heard them cry out, "I never saw it coming!" This quotation from Seneca speaks to that lack of preparation and warns against living with your head in the clouds.

Although many gurus today will tell you to only think positive thoughts in order to attract positive outcomes, the Stoics tell us that pessimism is actually conducive to a happy and fulfilling life. Contemporary philosopher Alain De Botton goes so far as to suggest that "Serenity ... begins with pessimism." This might sound completely foreign to our current societal attitudes. However, De Botton understands what the Stoics meant: By disappointing ourselves in a safe context, we can prepare ourselves for whatever the world might throw at us. De Botton advises, "We must learn to disappoint ourselves at leisure before the world ever has a chance to slap us by surprise at a time of its own choosing. The angry must learn to check their fury via a systematic, patient surrender of their more fervent hopes. They need to be carefully inducted to the darkest realities of life, to the stupidities of others, to the ineluctable failings of technology, to the necessary flaws of infrastructure. They should start each day with short yet thorough premeditation on the many humiliations and insults to which the coming hour's risk subsequently subjecting them."

However, negative visualization is not just about inoculating yourself against potential disappointment and stopping there. In fact, it can actually turn your life into the life of your dreams by helping you to understand that all these catastrophic things that you are envisioning have *not* actually happened to you. No matter what you are facing, you are comparatively lucky! Psychologists who study "anxious" people have discovered that the act of rehearsing all the possible negative consequences has a concrete, scientific benefit: it allows people to prepare their nervous systems, which means that when they do swing into action they will not be *over*-active and cause crippling panic attacks. This kind of foresight also helps encourage advance planning, which means that when the worst actually happens, you will be that much closer to a solution than people who never even entertained the possibility. So, if you can get the benefits of this "anxious" behavior without the pain of anxiety, why wouldn't you want to do it?

There are countless benefits of negative visualization. They include the ability to understand anxiety and to master it. Spending time contemplating the unknown allows us to train our minds and to protect it against uncertainty—like a vaccination that introduces small doses of a pathogen into the body. The constant exposure to negative images and ideas actually works to numb your mind to them. Think of negative visualization as a free mental training ground. Remember, according to Tim Ferris, "What we fear doing most is usually what we most need to do." This means that negative visualization can give us a roadmap that points to exactly what is holding us back and shows us the way forward. Furthermore, by creating realistic expectations, we avoid crushing disappointment. Finally, negative visualization makes us more grateful for what we do have. The end result is that it creates a healthy environment where it is possible—even easy!—for us to be our best selves.

Practical Advice and Tips for the Stoic Entrepreneur

How to Practice Negative Visualization

Negative visualization is a simple exercise that can remind us not to take the good things in our life for granted. In order to perform negative visualization, you just need to imagine that bad things have occurred or that good things have not happened. In order to prepare yourself to get all the benefits of this challenging practice, you need to find a quiet spot where you will not be disturbed. (When you get good at this, you will be able to do it anywhere, even in crowds. For now, as you are learning, make it as easy as possible.) Then, pick your worst fear. For example: imagine going bankrupt, the death of a dear friend, losing your spouse, or even experiencing a traumatic injury. Or, when you are about to start a new situation, imagine all the ways it could go wrong—we call this worst-case scenario thinking. For example, while you are on a boat, imagine that the ship is sinking and that everyone on it will drown (only do this if you are very tough). If you have stage fright, you might imagine your next presentation, and your Powerpoint slides do not work, and you lose your voice, and everyone starts laughing at you. Or imagine that you were born to a different set of parents and never met any of the people you love. In the case of your business, you can imagine that you lost all your clients, that you got caught in a terrible scandal, or that your office was vandalized. This will help you remember that everything you have is borrowed, another essential Stoic belief.

As you start to have these thoughts, try to feel them deep inside your entire body, all the way inside your skin and bones. Notice how they make you feel. Are you tensing up your muscles? Is your face making a pained expression? Do you forget to breathe deeply? Would someone watching you know what troubles you are experiencing inside of your mind? Now is the time to put your *apatheia* in action. The goal is not to avoid having emotions but to avoid being *controlled* by them.

Now, once you have mastered your emotions around the negative scenario, ask yourself what are the consequences if the worst really does happen? What is truly at stake for me and my business? Then, the next step is to ask yourself: am I ready to accept the consequences? How can I set up a plan to make sure to protect me from these possible consequences? More simply put: what is my safety net?

Then, when it comes time to prepare for your presentation, ask yourself: what would I do if my Powerpoint slides do not work? Can I bring a back-up copy? What about printouts? Can I present it from memory? Or, when you are deciding on renewing your office security plan or an insurance policy, spend some extra time discussing all the ways in which the plan or policy has you covered. With these simple precautions in place, you will be that much more confident when it comes time to tackle the actual challenge or traumatic event.

Stoic challenge: Practice Poverty

Tim Ferris, an American entrepreneur, and blogger recommends going even further and practicing poverty. This is his favorite stoic exercise that allows him to fully experience worst-case scenarios in a safe environment, rather than just playing them out in his imagination. He gets inspiration from a quote from Seneca that says, "It is precisely in times of immunity from care that the soul should toughen itself beforehand for occasions of greater stress, and it is while Fortune is kind that it should fortify itself against her violence. In days of peace, the soldier performs maneuvers, throws up earthworks with no enemy in sight, and wearies himself by gratuitous toil, in order that he may be equal to unavoidable toil." Tim Ferris recommends going beyond just mental rehearsals or journaling. Instead, he suggests setting at least three days in a row per month in which to fast, for example from Thursday evening to Sunday evening. If you are looking for a more advanced challenge, he recounts that a successful friend of his actually simulates poverty by living in poor conditions for an entire week. He sleeps in a sleeping bag in his own living room and tries to consume no more than $15 of food for the entire time. He does this once every financial quarter. This allows him to "better able to make decisions that are proactive and big picture, and less out of obligation, or guilt, or fear of missing out because he knows that even if he misses a particular deal, even if a cutting edge project or experiment, or his pushing the envelope fails, that he can make do and in fact, often thrive with next to nothing." Ferris notes that the experiment will serve to improve your mental and emotional state and although it feels unpleasant at the time, ultimately, it will be freeing. Aside from these extended scenarios like camping out or fasting, Ferris also does other things to cause himself pain and stress in a safe, controlled context, for instance, taking ice baths and suffering cold exposure. This allows him to develop a tolerance for the unavoidable challenges that life throws at everyone. He concludes, "The more you schedule and practice discomfort deliberately, the less unplanned discomfort will throw off your life and control your life."

Another way to "practice poverty" is to simply live a minimalist lifestyle, to begin with, and avoid getting enslaved by the attraction of riches. Emperor Marcus Aurelius supposedly sold many of the luxurious furnishings of his palace in order to pay down his empire's debt. He realized he did not need all his fancy luxuries, and that they were more of a burden for him and his people than a value. Today, we can see a similar mentality in some of the world's richest men. CEO Warren Buffett is worth approximately $65 billion, but he still lives in the exact same house he bought in 1958 for $31,500. Buffett does not do this because he is cheap. He does it because he knows what matters in life. He became successful precisely because of his commitment to prioritizing: for him, a standard house was better than a mega-mansion, because it allows him to focus his time on his work, rather than interior decorating. Maintaining this lifestyle actually gives him a kind of freedom to pursue what he truly loves. It also gives him a kind of insurance policy that he will always be able to be happy and satisfied even if there is a devastating financial crash—or if he experiences a debilitating injury and can never work again. Buffet understands that the more things people want and the more they have to do to earn or protect that lavish lifestyle, the less enjoyable their lives actually are, and the more constrained. Billionaire entrepreneur Mark Cuban also shares Buffett's frugality and tells people to cut out anything in their monthly budget that is not strictly essential. He claims, "The more you stress over bills, the more difficult it is to focus on your goals. The cheaper you can live, the greater your options."

Beyond just their everyday life, living frugally is a strategy that is celebrated and adopted by many entrepreneurs. The richest man in the world, Jeff Bezos, created Amazon around a frugal mentality. While some companies provide every possible luxury for their employees, Bezos argues, "I think frugality drives innovation, just like other constraints do. One of the only ways to get out of a tight box is to invent your way out.

Scheduling a Pre-mortem with your Team

A post-mortem is a traditional meeting in a business context where people get together to discuss how a project went, to evaluate whether it met the metrics for success and where to place the credit or the blame. This is similar to an autopsy, the moment went scientists figure out the cause of death (Latin: morte). Well, once the body is dead, the time for improvement has passed, so the Stoics would suggest, instead, scheduling a post-mortem with your team: that way you can try to figure out all the potential pitfalls that a project might face *before* they happen.

As a leader, it might be hard for you to stand in front of your team and expose your fears about a brand new project. But would you rather do that *before* they come to life—and hurt your bottom line—or after? As Seneca reminds us, "We are more often frightened than hurt; and we suffer more from imagination than from reality." So use this exercise as an opportunity to vanquish your fears, to block your imagination and to show your team what a fearless leader you are.

Do this exercise once you have mastered negative visualization, so you can explain it to the group. Gather them together and ask them to play devil's advocate as they outline all the steps of the next project. For each one, ask them to identify the worst-case scenario. Tell them to be creative but not absurd. Then ask them to write up a game plan for how to tackle these cases. What extra resources might you need to have? How much extra money? Will you need the help of an outside consultant? Could a partnership be beneficial? Go ahead and look up some of that contact information now, so you will not be rushing around trying to scramble and find the person when you already desperately need him.

Important note: If your business is doing well, do not be tempted to skip this exercise. Remember, Seneca, who enjoyed great wealth as Nero's adviser, warns us: "It is in times of security that the spirit should be preparing itself for difficult times; while fortune is bestowing favors on it is then is the time for it to be strengthened against her rebuffs." The last time you want to be practicing negative visualization is in the wake of a failure. Do it when you are riding high on success or even on an average day. It just might bring you down to earth—or remind you how good you have it.

Dealing with Adversity

So what happens when you have prepared for the worst and the worst still happens anyway? Sure, you can be an expert at negative visualization, you can even build the most intricate safety net imaginable, and you will still eventually come up against a disaster you never fathomed. Such is life.

This is the time when the stoic philosophy offers the most inspirational pearls of wisdom. First, remember you are in control of every single one of your choices, no matter how bad a situation you might face. As Epictetus said, "You can bind up my leg, but not even Zeus has the power to break my freedom of choice." Let a moment of adversity be the time when you recommit to living in alignment with your values and virtues.

Second, when working in a team, it is likely that the failure was caused by a combination of factors. It is rarely caused by one single weak person or one bad decision. As you are assessing the reasons for the failure in order to learn from it and grow, keep in mind Seneca's admonition: "Let philosophy scrape off your own faults, rather than be a way to rail against the faults of others." In simple terms, this means that you should use your training and experience as a way to look inwards at yourself, to identify your weaknesses and to improve them. This philosophical practice is not for casting the blame on others and refusing to look at yourself.

Third, never forget that we are made strong by our trials. Epictetus famously said, "Difficulty shows what men are. Therefore when a difficulty falls upon you, remember that God, like a trainer of wrestlers, has matched you with a rough young man. Why? So that you may become an Olympic conqueror, but it is not accomplished without sweat." So get up, dust yourself off, and figure out what comes next! If you need a little encouragement, take to heart the words of billionaire investor George Soros who says that "Once we realize that imperfect understanding is the human condition, there is no shame in being wrong, only in failing to correct our mistakes."

Furthermore, if it *is*, in fact, another person who has caused the adversity, this is an excellent opportunity for tapping into the best of Stoicism. The popular blogger, Tim Urban, had this to say to one of his readers who asked him the simple question, "How do you be a good person?" He suggested that she keep in mind the following, in order to be a kinder, more empathetic person:

"Every stranger, co-worker, friend, acquaintance, customer service representative, driver, waiter, customer, client, neighbor, and person on the internet you come across:

- Has a family who loves them and vice versa
- Has hopes and dreams and regrets and frustrations
- Has as many thoughts going through their head at all times as you do
- Is dealing with random health problems, trying to make ends meet financially, and is probably tired
- Might be supporting one or more other human beings
- Might be just a little sad all the time about a tragedy in their past
- Might be the most important person in someone else's life
- Is just trying to figure out how to be happy"

In today's fast-paced world, where communication is often anonymous and frequently aggressive and careless, keep these thoughtful guidelines in mind. Urban's suggestion about how to be good touches on the concept of "sympatheia," or interconnectedness amongst human beings. We will discuss that more in Chapter 6. For now, just think about these salient points whenever you encounter adversity that is caused by another person, whether by his careless error or overt malice.

Do not forget, your journal is the most valuable tool to help you achieve these difficult objectives. (Are you still writing in it twice every day? Do not stop! Keep making deposits in that bank of knowledge!) Use it to describe whatever challenges you are facing. As you write, see if you can achieve a stoic mindset and extract the best possible lesson from any negative outcome, no matter how big. Then, remind yourself exactly what is and what is not in your control. For instance, you might even divide up a single story according to what is and is not in your control: I went to the store (in my control), but it was closed (not in my control). So I didn't have dinner (in my control) and at bedtime, I ended up eating a bunch of junk food (in my control). Then look back at what you wrote and see if you can pinpoint the exact moment you went wrong—for instance, in this case, it was letting the closed store derail your plan for healthy eating. Do not dwell on it, just make a note and try to plan to do better next time. You can write down: check the store schedule before going, find another open store, always make sure to shop *before* I run out of groceries, have a healthy take-out place in mind for when I can't shop, etc.

The first three chapters helped prepare us to get us into the stoic mindset. Now, in the next chapter, we will tackle the essential topic of how to use stoicism to get ourselves into action—which is the foundational principle of stoicism. Together, you can harness motivation, discipline, and productivity in order to get your business into the most dynamic, impactful shape possible.

Summary: The Chapter In Brief

Along with journaling, one of the cornerstones in stoic philosophy is negative visualization (*premeditation malorum*). This practice, which involves mentally confronting our worst fears, can help lessen anxiety by immunizing us against it. Beyond the mental comfort it provides, negative visualization also allows us to prepare for an event in advance to make sure we have a safety net for whatever worst-case scenario life might throw at us. For the business person, this is essential because of the countless responsibilities you will certainly have to juggle. At its most basic, negative visualization increases happiness because it stimulates appreciation and gratitude for what we do have. It reminds us not to sweat the small stuff. The chapter also recommends scheduling a post-mortem with your entire team before embarking on any major projects, in order to stem any potential pitfalls and prepare a backup plan. Finally, it reminds you that adversity is an inevitable part of a successful, daring life, so take the challenge for what it is and make it part of your process of growth, development, and improvement.

Chapter 3: Get to Work, Stoic. How to use Stoicism to Increase Motivation, Cultivate Discipline, and Enhance Productivity

"The chief task in life is simply this: to identify and separate matters so that I can say clearly to myself which are externals under my control, and which have to do with the choices I actually control. Where then do I look for good and evil? Not to uncontrollable externals, but within myself to the choices that are my own..."

-Epictetus

Stoicism is a philosophy that values action, but what happens when you are plagued with doubt to the point where you are unable to make decisions? (Think: Hamlet's "to be or not to be...") This can hinder every aspect of your business, sapping you of your needed motivation and halting your productivity. For Epictetus, good and evil can only be found in the decisions we make, which means that by lacking the willpower and confidence to make decisions, we lose the opportunity to live a virtuous life.

As we discussed in the previous chapter, the power to make choices is a cornerstone of Stoicism. (Recall the striking quotation by Epictetus, who said, "You can bind up my leg, but not even Zeus has the power to break my freedom of choice.") In fact, stoics go so far as to believe that our choices are literally the only thing that matters—because they are the only thing fully under our control.

So once we decide what to do, how do we pass to the action phase and actually get things done? Luckily, the Stoics have a lot to say on the topics of increasing motivation, cultivating discipline and enhancing productivity. After we look at some stoic wisdom on that topic, we will consider their perspective on what is supposed to happen afterward: taking responsibility for whatever outcome occurs and persevering in spite of the odds.

Tips for Increasing Motivation

Stoicism is a unique philosophy because it stands for decisive action, and not for passive contemplation. A stoic cannot simply wait for inspiration to strike him, he must be his own inspiration. One of the best examples of this philosophy is summed up in the pithy statement of Epictetus who once said, "First say to yourself what you would be, and then do what you have to do."

Often the biggest challenge we face when actually getting down to work is the distraction of the world around us. Our cell phones and computers blast notifications about every single news event on the entire planet. Our friends text us at all hours of the day. Advertisers want to grab onto our wallets. Quite simply, a successful entrepreneur does not have time for these distractions. Usually, these distractions end up making us feel bad. We learn about devastating global tragedies we have no power to stop, or we feel inadequate compared to the perfect picture that marketers try to sell us. As Marcus Aurelius teaches us, the answer to this problem is to look internally: "If you are distressed by anything external, the pain is not due to the thing itself, but to your estimate of it; and this you have the power to revoke at any moment."

In order to face these distractions, we recommend creating a plan for your day, with set routines and rituals to help you get through. Using your journal as a guide, you can start to automate your daily activities, so you no longer have to struggle to decide when you will answer your millions of work emails: you will just sit down and answer them during the scheduled time. (And, of course, remember to delegate the ones that are not important.)

Perhaps the greatest bit of stoic wisdom surrounding the issue of motivation is this simple thought from Marcus Aurelius about the brevity of life. How true is it when he writes, "You could leave life right now. Let that determine what you do and say and think." Or, in the wise words of Seneca, "While we wait for life, life passes."

Tips for Cultivating Stoic Discipline

Every single one of the previous activities discussed in the earlier chapters can and should be part of your stoic discipline. After trying them all out, you will be able to see which ones work best for you. Then you can adapt them to your personal lifestyle and business goals. In this section, we discuss the value of discipline itself, regardless of what it is being directed towards. These principles can be effective for tackling any challenge in your life, whether it is getting into better physical shape, finally finishing a challenging home improvement project or learning a brand new foreign language. Of course, we will want to focus on the business aspects here, but keep these other possibilities in mind, too. After all, the more disciplined you are in general, the better off you will be. If you are a paragon of precision in the office and then come home and cannot manage to cook yourself a healthy meal or go to the gym, you will eventually suffer in your work life too! Remember: No one ever lived their best life without a conscientious fitness regime, including diet, exercise, stretching and proper rest.

If you need more motivation to cultivate discipline, we leave you with this powerful quote about why an action, self-mastery, and control are the most important tools for living a happy, virtuous life. Seneca writes: "Putting things off is the biggest waste of life: it snatches away each day as it comes, and denies us the present by promising the future. The greatest obstacle to living is expectancy, which hangs upon tomorrow and loses today. You are arranging what lies in fortune's control, and abandoning what lies in yours. What are you looking at? To what goal are you straining? The whole future lies in uncertainty: live immediately."

Tips for Enhancing Productivity

Of course, there is no sense in living immediately if you are just flailing around. Only act after you have cultivated a strategic plan for what comes next—based on where you want to go. Do you want to be in charge of every single tiny aspect of your business? If you answered yes, you might be a perfectionist and, quite possibly, also a control freak. If this is the case, then this advice is especially for you.

When running a business, the most important thing to do is as little as necessary. Not as little as possible, but as little as necessary. Why is this? Because what is truly needed for your business is your big-picture vision. You are not running a business because of your photocopying skills (although maybe they are great) or because you can write a great email. Do less. Automate what you can. That is what technology (and a skilled personal assistant) is for. Delegate what you can't. Then you will be able to focus on what is truly important and maximize your efficiency.

If you are not quite at the stage where you can afford secretarial or administrative assistance, do not despair. Your time will come. In the meantime, use these activities to cultivate another important stoic practice. Visualize the process you are undertaking and see all the interconnectedness even of something incredibly small. Maybe you are photocopying handouts for your upcoming budget presentation. Imagine your prospective clients looking through those handouts and realizing what a talented speaker you are (you can also imagine that they hate the handouts as part of a negative visualization and then inspire yourself to make them even better). Maybe you are sending out fifty Linkedin connection requests in order to meticulously build up your network. As you tediously hit the "send" button over and over again, try to imagine one of them reaching the person who will connect you to the client of your dreams. Then the repetitive act of clicking "send" will not seem so tiresome but instead will feel like an interconnected part of a bigger journey. As you go through this process, always remember what is under your control and keep your eyes on the big picture.

The Importance of Taking Responsibility for the Outcome

Anyone who has spent any time in the real world knows that it is true that we are all interconnected. Even the smallest decision of whether to angrily honk your horn at a careless driver can have repercussions that go beyond what you can immediately see. This sense of interconnectedness gives us a responsibility to think about the consequences of every decision we make. It is particularly true for you as an entrepreneur, as you constantly have to assess those around you to make decisions that will impact their lives and your company. You must decide: whom should you hire? Whom should you partner with? To whom should you entrust your finances? With whom should you sign a lease? And, when something goes wrong, the natural question to ask is: whom should I blame? Naturally, your mind might go to the interrelated web of circumstances that led you to a bad business partner or an unscrupulous accountant or an unfair landlord. Stoicism tells us to focus on someone else: yourself.

More precisely, since we want to remove ourselves from the mindset of blame and praise, stoicism tells us that you should take responsibility for whatever happens that is within your control. Seneca has wise words about how Stoic philosophy can help us achieve this. He reminds us: "Let philosophy scrape off your own faults, rather than be a way to rail against the faults of others." With these words in mind, do not be afraid of standing in front of your team and acknowledging your responsibility for a major failure. If you have laid the groundwork, then you perfectly understand where you wanted to go and why. Therefore, you will be able to understand your part in the failed journey, if not immediately then with some time for reflection. Most importantly, you will be able to right the course as quickly as possible and to lead your team back on the correct path (or to change the path based on what you experienced and learned). Learning from your mistakes makes you a tough leader, not a weak one, but first, you have to acknowledge that those mistakes were yours, to begin with.

How to Persevere In Spite of the Odds

When something goes wrong in your personal business, it can be heartbreaking. You put everything you have into a project—your time, your money, your passion—and you bring others along with you for the ride. When you hit a bump in the road, Stoicism offers trenchant advice about how to handle it. Marcus Aurelius once wrote, "Everything that happens is either endurable or not. If it's endurable, then endure it. Stop complaining. If it's unendurable... then stop complaining. Your destruction will mean its end as well. Just remember: you can endure anything your mind can make endurable, by treating it as in your interest to do so." From this perspective, no matter what the situation, the course of action is the same: stop complaining. All you need to do is to work on your mindset and go forward. Seneca said something similar but in much fewer words. This could be a good mantra to post above your workspace or on your night table: "It does not matter what you bear, but how you bear it."

Remember, perseverance does not mean stubbornly doing the same thing over and over again regardless of what happens. Yes, it is important to have a vision and to stay committed to it, but a stoic must also always be observing his surroundings and his reality. Sometimes persevering means pivoting to another idea when the original plan proves faulty. Flexibility and adaptability are important qualities in a leader as well—and show connectedness with the reality that the Stoics argued was essential to living a virtuous life.

Practical Advice and Tips for the Stoic Entrepreneur

1. Write down post-it notes with your goals, and cover your mirror with so you are forced to look at them every day. Put the most important ones in the center where your face should be so that you can recognize you are blocking out your true self by not striving towards these fundamental goals as soon as possible.
2. Find one thing every day that you can do *less* of, whether by automating it or delegating it or simply letting it go. Remember, a tiny daily change adds up to a lot. Are you answering every insignificant email? Wasting time on social media? Shopping for bargains that cost you more in time than they save you for money? Stop, stop, stop.
3. Look back over your journal. Is there some issue or challenge that you keep putting off? Time's up! Commit yourself to do it immediately—or pay the consequences. (Research shows that penalizing yourself for bad behavior is very effective in motivating people to get things done. Pick something that really hurts: tell yourself you will have to give up your favorite tv show or skip taking the elevator and

climb the stairs every day at the office. There are even online sites that will do this for you, for instance, donating money to a charity you hate, if you do not live up to a self-commitment!)

Summary: The Chapter In Brief

Chapter 4 takes the stoic principles and tells you how to start living in your everyday life. No more delays. Once you have figured out what is under your control, it is time to make big decisions and take concrete action. This chapter detailed how to increase your motivation, cultivate strong discipline and enhance your productivity. Then it gives some tips about what to do after you have taken action: taking responsibility for any outcome and keeping on with your work, even when things do not go right. Remember it is all just training for future success.

Chapter 4: The Stoic in the World: How to Stoicism Can Improve Self-Confidence, Communication with Others and Make You a Better Negotiator

"If you hear that someone is speaking ill of you, instead of trying to defend yourself you should say: 'He obviously does not know me very well, since there are so many other faults he could have mentioned'." — *Epictetus*

This quotation by Epictetus makes a perfect start to chapter five because it combines the two interrelated topics we will cover here: how to combine honest self-reflection (introspection) with fair evaluations of others (extrospection). First, we will discuss how each of these ideas is to be used in Stoic philosophy, and then we will conclude by exploring how you can bring them together for the benefit of your business. By understanding yourself and knowing how to analyze those around you, the end result will be that you will become a better negotiator.

The brilliance of Epictetus' quotation lies in the set-up. It starts by referring to a common problem or fear, the fear of negative judgment from those who surround us. The usual knee-jerk defense in response to such negative rumors would be to undermine the person's authority by saying, "He obviously does not know me very well." Epictetus starts to follow this logic, but then he quickly turns the tables in the last part of the quotation, when he adds, "since there are so many other faults he could have mentioned." Now, our critic's authority has, in fact, been undermined, but not because he was *too* critical of us, but because he was *ignorant* of all our flaws that only we have access to. Genius!

Building Self-Confidence and Self-Awareness (introspection)

Stoicism is fundamentally an introspective practice. Introspection, defined as the "Observation or examination of one's own emotional state, men tal processes, etc.; the act of

looking within "oneself" is at the heart of all the practices we have discussed so far in this book. As we discussed in chapter 2 on journaling and chapter 3 on negative visualization, the stoic looks inside himself constantly, day and night, week after week. As we discussed in chapter 4, he takes responsibility for the outcomes of his choices and always works diligently on his self-improvement.

The benefit of this self-awareness is, first and foremost, self-confidence. If you know what you are, then you know exactly what you can do. You can walk into a meeting in front of the richest venture capitalists in the world, and tell them exactly why they should trust you with their hard-earned money. And you can have the confidence to walk away from a deal if it does not seem favorable—or if it is not in line with your values. Furthermore, if you know who you are, you know *why* you do what you do. The famous and talented Elon Musk, one of the most successful entrepreneurs the world has ever known, rates daily introspection as one of the most important things a person can do. He says, "I think that's the single best piece of advice: Constantly think about how you could be doing things better and questioning yourself."

Of course, it will sound paradoxical, but one of the key tools for introspection is actually to look to another respected person. As Seneca suggested, "Choose someone whose way of life as well as words, and whose very face as mirroring the character that lies behind it, have won your approval. Be always pointing him out to yourself either as your guardian or as your model. This is a need, in my view, for someone as a standard against which our characters can measure themselves. Without a ruler to do it against you will not make the crooked straight." This "ruler" could be a peer or a mentor—perhaps it is the very person who inspired you to go into business, to begin with. It also could be a person from the past (like a Stoic) or a celebrity. So keep your mind open to learning about new people, read biographies, and you will find your ideal "ruler." At the same time, make sure not to follow anyone blindly or singularly; after all, even the most perfect of idols can fall, like some of the apparent business greats of the twentieth century (we could mention Bernie Madoff and Elizabeth Holmes, just to name two).

The Benefits of an Awareness of Others (extrospection)

The Stoics teach that you should only worry about what you control, and in the opening quotation from Epictetus, we talked about the idea that *you* are your own toughest, truest critic. So where does that leave other people?? The dictionary defines extrospection as "the observation of things external to one's own mind...Extrospection is ordinary sense perception or reasoning concerning the things so perceived." But if stoicism is so focused on the self and its improvement, why should we also practice extrospection?

Well, because Stoicism is a practical, pragmatic philosophy, concerned primarily with action. Therefore, in this interconnected world, it is impossible to just focus on the self. We have to remember we are connected to every other thing on the planet, living and nonliving. In order to make informed decisions, you can't just go inside yourself completely, except during the precious daily moments of meditation (so make them count!). Instead, you need to interact with the world around you, for several reasons.

1) Through the consideration and observation of things external to the self, we are more likely to gain a valuable perspective on what to do in our lives and in our business. This might mean studying the great businessmen and women we admire, the heroes of the distant past, or even our colleagues and friends.
2) Extrospection gives us perspective about our role in the larger picture, which helps avoid a tragic self-centered disposition. When we observe the world around us, we realize how small we are, and how similar we are to our fellow men and women. This makes our perception of tragic, unique suffering much more proportional.
3) Extrospection gives us both something to strive for—and something to avoid.
4) Extrospection helps us evaluate possible friends, colleagues, and business partners. As Seneca reminds us,

"Associate with people who are likely to improve you. Welcome those who you are capable of improving. The process is a mutual one: men learn as they teach." Berkshire Hathaway CEO Warren Buffett, probably the most successful businessman of contemporary history, suggests a similar approach: "It's better to hang out with people better than you. Pick out associates whose behavior is better than yours and you'll drift in that direction." This means we must truly study those with whom we wish to spend time. Ask yourself: do they align with my values? Remember, no one is perfect, so consider: Will they help me improve myself? Can they learn from me?

Finally, when evaluating people, keep in mind what Seneca said: "There is no genius without a touch of madness." The people you might admire most will also likely have some flaws. Since you are (or want to be) an entrepreneur, the same can probably be said about you!

How to Deal with Anger and Disappointment

When dealing with others as a result of extrospection, you will inevitably have positive experiences and negative ones, too. The Stoics teach that we should neither get carried away by the good or by the bad, so remember not to let your feelings run away with you, even if you think you have found the ideal business partner or employee. Always keep in control of your emotions.

Negative emotions tend to be harder to deal with, so we will spend more time talking about self-mastery in this regard, specifically in terms of the powerful emotions of anger and disappointment. Marcus Aurelius had wise words of inspiration to help discourage anger. He writes, "Keep this thought handy when you feel a fit of rage coming on—it isn't manly to be enraged. Rather, gentleness and civility are more human, and therefore manlier. A real man doesn't give way to anger and discontent, and such a person has strength, courage, and endurance—unlike the angry and complaining. The nearer a man comes to a calm mind, the closer he is to strength." Today, we could rewrite his passage and say that it applies to either men or women because anger is unbecoming in both sexes. Always try to keep in mind your ultimate goal and remember that it will not be reached by flying off the handle and acting rashly. In fact, you are more likely to destroy all your hard work if people see you as unpredictable; a trustworthy leader knows how to be calm in a storm.

Moreover, if you have been practicing your negative visualization, you will be well prepared to face disappointment, because that is one of its primary benefits: to consider the worst possible outcome of a situation so that your expectations do not come crashing to the ground when they are not met. Try this practice when imagining a new working relationship: imagine that an employee has done the worst job imaginable, and then think about what plans you have in place as a safeguard against such possible mistakes. This should be a good first step to relaxing you. Remember, when you have finished the visualization, shake off any remaining negative feelings, so that your working relationship with the person stays neutral and controlled.

The contemporary philosopher Alain de Botton, who has written extensively (and critically) about Stoicism, suggests that learning to disappoint yourself can be a powerful way to deal with anger. He refers to a quotation by Seneca that says, "What need is there to weep over parts of life? The whole of it calls for tears." De Botton argues that the Stoics help us put things into perspective. For example, he writes, "We may be irritated that it is raining, but we are unlikely ever to respond to a shower by screaming. We aren't overwhelmed by anger whenever we are frustrated; we are sent into a rage only when we first allowed ourselves to believe in a hopeful scenario which was then dashed suddenly and apparently without warning. Our greatest furies spring from unfortunate events which we had not factored into our vision of reality." De Botton sees Stoic pessimism as a safeguard against anger and, in fact, a path towards happiness. Optimism, on the other hand, is actually what ends up getting us to travel down a dark path because it led us to be foolish in our expectations, to hope for more than what was smart or realistic. He writes, "The person who shouts every time they encounter a traffic jam betrays a faith, at once touching and demented, that roads must always be (mysteriously) traffic-free. The person who loses their temper with every new employee or partner evinces a curious belief that a perfection is an option for the human animal." So really, from this perspective, optimism is a form of self-delusion, while pessimism is the kind of pragmatic realism that can make us stronger and better able to engage the world around us.

Stoic Negotiation Tactics

If we have looked into ourselves and examined others, we are ready to bring ourselves into contact with our potential negotiators. But what can stoicism tell us about how to succeed in business negotiations, one of the most challenging but vital aspects of entrepreneurship?

First, we must carefully prepare ourselves for the encounter. This is done bit by bit in the daily work of stoic practices, but make sure to intensify the practice when you are getting near to a major negotiation. Enter into the negotiation with a clear goal.

Know what you will accept and what you will not. Have clear boundaries and commit to respecting them in the letter. Remember Seneca's words, "If a person doesn't know to which port they sail, no wind is favorable." So keep your destination in front of your mind.

Second, try to put yourself in the mind of the person with whom you are negotiating (notice we did not write "adversary"—more on that soon). This can be easier if you have been practicing extrospection and have had a chance to observe him, his colleagues or his employees. If not, try an online search to see what you can find out. Maybe you have mutual acquaintances. Be discrete, but make sure to do your homework. Then, on the morning of the negotiation, wake up and remind yourself, as Marcus Aurelius counseled, "Begin each day by telling yourself: Today I shall be meeting with interference, ingratitude, insolence, disloyalty, ill-will, and selfishness..."

Third, when you enter into the actual negotiation, let the other person speak longer and, preferably, first. The more information you have gathered about him, the easier this will be. And, if you have not managed to get too much background on him, by letting him talk during the negotiation, you gather valuable data. On the subject of speaking up—and staying quiet—Cato had these smart words; he wrote, "I begin to speak only when I'm certain what I'll say isn't better left unsaid." If you keep your cool, speak knowledgeably and with confidence, and keep your destination in mind, you will be likely to get what you want.

Finally, in the next chapter, we will be discussing the concept of interconnectedness, but we will preview it here, as it is relevant to negotiation. The Stoics tell us to always remember that everyone is interconnected, like threads in woven cloth or parts of a single body. If you keep that in mind, then the best piece of stoic advice for negotiation is to not see the other person as an adversary. Instead, think of him as a fellow human, all part of the interconnected web of life. Think of him as a fellow businessman who has his own goals and dreams and his own bottom line. Can you find a mutually agreeable solution that does not compromise either of your values? Can you find a workable compromise that will lead to future collaboration and growth? That would truly be "winning" in the Stoic sense.

Practical Advice and Tips for the Stoic Entrepreneur

1. Are you still doing your morning and evening journaling exercises every single day? If you have stopped, make sure to pick them back up immediately. There is no better defense against all the challenges of the modern world than self-knowledge.

2. As part of your journaling, try to write objective sketches of the people around you in your business life: colleagues, competitors, potential clients. Limit yourself to what you objectively know about each one of them. Do not let your emotions or biases enter the picture. Imagine these people were being studied by alien scientists: how would they each look to someone who only saw them from the outside?

3. Get angry (but only for five minutes). Psychologists recommend a habit in which you experience a difficult emotion for a short period of time in a contained setting. This is similar to negative visualization, but instead, it concentrates specifically on whatever emotion is troubling you today, whether anger or disappointment or fear. Set a timer, close your eyes, and think of something that triggers that emotion in you. You may yell or gesture or do anything that comes naturally to you. You might punch a pillow or let out a stream of foul language. Then, when the timer goes off, you must stop and return back to your normal calm state as quickly as possible. Think about how that intense experience made you feel. Did you like the feeling of your blood pressure and heart rate skyrocketing? Did you like the surge of adrenaline—

maybe only for a second. As the feeling subsides with deep breaths, notice how much better you feel after you let the feeling go. Next time you encounter that emotion in your daily life, try to recognize the signs more quickly and revert to the slow, deep breathing rather than exploding and letting your emotions take over. Remember, that by rationally communicating your feelings (telling someone, "I feel angry") rather than swallowing them and hoping they disappear, you will be better positioned to obtain self-mastery.

Advanced practice: after mastering this controlled anger, remember the suggestion of contemporary philosopher Alain De Botton, "One of the goals of civilization is to instruct us in how to be sad rather than angry. Sadness may not sound very appealing. But it carries—in this context—a huge advantage. It is what allows us to detach our emotional energies from fruitless fury around things that (however bad) we cannot change and that is the fault of no one in particular and—after a period of mourning—to refocus our efforts in places where our few remaining legitimate hopes and expectations have a realistic chance of success." Therefore, after mastering your anger, try this exercise again, but with sadness: do a negative visualization with the goal of conjuring up all the tears within you, and let them freely flow as you imagine all the things you cannot change and all the terrible things that could happen to you. Feel where your body experiences sadness, and then breathe into those spots. When the timer goes off, practice returning to a perfectly calm state and continuing on your day. Try this every day for a week or month and see how much lighter you feel in your daily existence.

4. In the days leading up to negotiation, try to practice this exercise several times a day: do a negative visualization in which you imagine every step of the negotiation. Visualize the room you are in, what you are wearing, what you are going to ask for, and what they will want in return. Now imagine each part of this process going terribly wrong. Imagine the room being 100 degrees hot, imagine the other person refusing to listen to you, or being greedy or rude. Feel your body react and then take deep breaths until you return to calm and to composure.

5. If you are really nervous about negotiation, ask a trusted friend to do a practice round with you. If you have done exercise 2 above and created a character sketch about the person with whom you will be negotiating, let him read it and ask him to get into character. Practice negotiating until your body and mind are completely at ease with the interaction.

6. After the negotiation, do not forget to write down what happened, good and bad. Then make notes about where you would like to improve and save them for review before the next negotiation takes place.

Summary: The Chapter In Brief

Chapter five discusses how introspection and extrospection work to put you in the strongest possible position as an entrepreneur. By knowing yourself and others, as used in Stoic philosophy, you can bring them together for the benefit of your business. One key way that this will help you is in your ability to manage your anger and disappointment. Finally, knowing your strengths and weaknesses—and those of your fellow businessmen!—is key to one of the foundational business skills: negotiating.

Chapter 5: Practical Examples of how Interconnectedness can help you relate to employees, partners, clients and improve your well being

"All things are mutually woven together and therefore have an affinity for each other," Marcus Aurelius

One of the most powerful changes in mindset that you can bring to your new or established business is a recognition of what Marcus Aurelius calls "interconnectedness" or *sympatheia* (which sounds quite like the English "sympathy" but has a more subtle meaning). In this chapter, we will talk about how to deal with different kinds of people in business and different business relationships, such as employees, business partners, and clients. However, the underlying principle that unifies each one of these groups is this crucial notion of interdependence. Just like threads in a piece of fabric, each one of the people you interact with your business is part of your business, whether it is the parking lot attendant, the customer service representative who helps you troubleshoot a difficult task, or your closest, oldest confidant. Each one of those people is like the different parts of the body, each with his or her own function and objective, but each integral to the health of the organism. Whenever you encounter difficulties with someone, remember this principle of *sympatheia,* and your interaction will become all the more meaningful and potentially even healing.

How to Deal with Poor Performance in Employees

If you have any employees at all, even if yours are the most diligent, you will eventually have to deal with the unpleasant reality of their poor performance. How you handle their poor performance will have powerful repercussions throughout your business; it will send a message to the other employees and, without exaggeration, it will ultimately determine if your business is to succeed or to fail.

Although sometimes it can be extremely frustrating—or even traumatic—when an employee messes up, the first thing the Stoics tell us to do is to avoid getting angry, as we know that anger is one of the most powerful distractions for the human mind. It clouds our best judgment, and it makes us behave against our core values. Seneca wrote a lengthy essay on anger. In it, he provides some helpful tips for how to avoid getting angry when an employee does not perform. He tells us: "the best plan is to reject straightway the first incentives to anger, to resist its very beginnings, and to take care not to be betrayed into it: for if once it begins to carry us away, it is hard to get back again into a healthy condition, because reason goes for nothing when once passion has been admitted to the mind, and has by our own free will been given a certain authority, it will for the future do as much as it chooses, not only as much as you will allow it. The enemy, I repeat, must be met and driven back at the outermost frontier-line: for when he has once entered the city and passed its gates, he will not allow his prisoners to set bounds to his victory." Here, it may be helpful to remember philosopher Alain De Botton's comment about the power of pessimism and the danger of optimism when dealing with other people. He writes: "The person who loses their temper with every new employee or partner evinces a curious belief that a perfection is an option for the human animal." So always repeat to yourself that perfection is an illusion and imperfection is the human condition, and you will be well on your way to dealing with employee mistakes calmly.

Hopefully, you are able to take this advice and avoid letting anger into your mind and suppress your rationality. However, if you have not yet learned this form of self-control, make sure you do not engage the employee in an angry, emotional state. Step away if necessary. Once you are calm, you must carefully evaluate the situation. Ask yourself: What kind of mistake did the employee make? Was it her first mistake of this kind? Did she do everything in her power to get help before the problem occurred? Did she report her problems to the necessary supervisor? If so, she probably can learn from her mistakes. In this case, it is your job as an employer to ensure she has the proper support so that it does not happen again. This might mean installing "guard rails" within your company to make sure employees are being helped at crucial phases, without, of course, having their work done for them. This is what hedge fund manager Ray Dalio does with his employees at Bridgewater, when necessary. As this process unfolds, make sure not to get angry at the employee, which according to the Stoics is our duty. If we can better the employee through teaching him and creating new procedures (that do not put your budget in jeopardy, of course), it is your duty to do so. This pedagogical approach will not only improve the individual but ultimately benefit the company—and even society—as a whole.

However, if you evaluate the situation and find out that the employee was trying to hide some sort of weakness or was being lazy, it might be time to terminate the relationship. Similarly, if he knew he was having problems but refused to ask for help, or has committed repeated errors of the same kind, it might also be time to let him go. Remember, your organization is like a body and each part contributes to its success—or could prove to be a fatal weakness (what the Greeks called an Achilles heel). As the boss, you have to evaluate whether rehabilitation of the employee will be possible and efficient—or perhaps they belong in a different role inside the company, if their talents aren't being used to their fullest in their current role. This is an ideal solution, but make sure you are not just relocating them to avoid a painful conversation. You may want to get additional information from other colleagues and supervisors, always being careful to weigh the advice and account for potential biases. But, if after you have conducted a thorough, rational investigation, you find out that they do not have anything to offer the company in any department, then do not be afraid to terminate a poorly performing employee. Being kind and looking the other way ultimately hurts the company, the other employees and you. Whether or not you believe it, it even hurts the employee himself. It is better for him to look himself honestly in the mirror and figure out what line of work he should really be in—and the sooner, the better!

Once you have dealt with the problem, the organism should be able to heal itself quickly. Furthermore, if you are transparent about your processes, about employee performance reviews, transfers, and terminations, no one will be afraid of their own job, because they will know exactly what to expect. Remember, leadership guru Brené Brown encourages those good leaders to avoid fostering a workplace where people gossip because no one thrives in an office full of backstabbing and scheming colleagues. Remember that the enemy to corruption is light, so shed light on what you are doing as the head of your organization—and remove those who seek to keep the organization in the dark. They are always doing so for their own best interests, never yours.

Finally, one last word of advice: if you do a thorough job in the hiring process, you will be much less likely to encounter employees performing poorly. This means to create a hiring process that is transparent and in-depth, with multiple kinds of interviews and tests that are evaluated in a standard way across the company. If you do your own hiring, you can spend time asking the candidate questions about his values and assessing his sincerity and his alignment with company values. If you have hiring managers, make sure *they* are in alignment with company values. Have a strict, well-defined rubric that covers all the areas a candidate must address during his on-site visit. If you trust them, ask them to draft a set of guidelines that you can revise together to make sure you're on the same page. More importantly, ask the hiring managers to do blind reviews of the candidate and forward them to you without comparing their results with other hiring managers. Before the candidate's visit, spend time with the hiring managers in formal and informal situations to make sure they know what to look for in an ideal (preferably stoic!) employee. And unless your company is over 1,000 employees, make sure you spend at least fifteen minutes with a top-level candidate before he gets the formal offer. If you have been doing your stoic exercises carefully, you will be able to assess their potential fit, in even the briefest of meetings.

How to Improve Relationships with Business Partners

So how does stoicism help you when dealing with colleagues? Business partners cannot be treated as employees because they do not answer to you. Instead, they must work with you in the most efficient possible way, for the benefit of all considered. In many ways, the same advice about employees above applies to business partners, in terms of understanding the symbiotic relationship between all people. Quite literally, you and your partners are interconnected, and your success is interdependent.

But what happens when you face inevitable disagreements? You probably picked your business partners because of their fast-thinking, independence and innovative attitude—which means you are likely to disagree at some point. Here, Marcus Aurelius has some great advice about what to do in case of such a disagreement. He writes, "If someone is able to show me that what I think or do is not right, I will happily change, for I seek the truth, by which no one was ever truly harmed. It is the person who continues in his self-deception and ignorance who is harmed."

The good news is since we are all interconnected, it does not matter who is right—all that matters is that you get to the truth, however long it might take. Of course, sooner is better, so when dealing with business partners and disagreements, keep an open mind and an open heart. If multiple smart, disinterested, and fair people disagree with you, you should take extra caution before dismissing their advice. Ask yourself why do you think they are telling you these things? (This same advice holds if an employee gets the courage to tell you he thinks you are wrong. Obviously, he is taking a big risk in confronting you.) Ask yourself: is this someone whose opinion I value on this matter? If so, give him the benefit of the doubt and listen—it just might change the course of your business!

On the other hand, if you are sincerely convinced that you are truly right, based on careful evaluation of all possible evidence, then Marcus Aurelius has a different piece of advice. He advised that people should be" kind and good-natured to everyone, and ready to show this particular person the nature of his error." For the Stoics, improving a single individual actually benefits the entire society, and so being a good mentor is a highly virtuous endeavor. It may take a lot of time and effort, but keep in mind all the benefits it is generating, some of which might be hidden to you in the present moment. In any case, do your best, but try not to get too caught up in teaching others to follow your ways. Remember, if it were really that easy to teach someone the Stoic way of life, the world would be a much better place, so possibly the best advice on dealing with querulous business partners is Marcus Aurelius' suggestion: "Waste no more time arguing what a good man should be, be one."

Negotiation and Selling

Chapter 5 looked at how stoicism can help you improve your negotiation strategies, and here we will go a little deeper into the topic and also think about how stoicism can help you make a sale. Here are a few of the ways that Stoicism can help you in your dealings with other vendors or clients. First, the regular daily practices should significantly increase your confidence. This means that you know that you are going into a negotiation prepared with a clear goal in mind. Second, thanks to the self-awareness you gain from doing twice daily journaling meditations, you should know your best strengths and your major weaknesses. This means that you can present yourself or your product in the most flattering possible light and downplay any limitations it might have. Third, since you will have learned to control your passions, you will be able to play it cool no matter what the other person says or does to you. Fourth, because you will remember that everyone is interconnected, you will behave respectfully and justly to everyone, because the person to whom you are selling or with whom you are negotiating also has his own bottom line, his own principles, and his own ideals. (Even if you cannot see what they are at the present.) Finally, thanks to Stoicism, you will have learned detachment from the outcome. This means you recognize that as soon as you start to desire a specific result, you always lose, even if it may sound paradoxical. Obviously, if you do not get what you want, you lose. However, even if you *do* get what you want, Stoics believes you lose anyway because the thing you have obtained will change or you yourself will change. This does not mean to be resigned to accept whatever might come, but to strive to follow nature in your business as in everything, which will ultimately lead to the proper result.

How to Improve Your Relationship with Your Clients

Especially when starting our business, our clients are the people we crave most to bring into our life. After all, with no clients, there is no business. Or, when your business grows, if your client base does not grow sufficiently, you will fear to have trouble bringing in Venture Capitalists. In these early growth phases, we must be extra attentive to only be associating with those people that bring out the best in us. Do not be tempted to just accept *any* client who pulls out a checkbook. If you do that, you will increase your likelihood of problems later on, when inevitably something goes wrong—or when your values simply clash with your clients. If you are operating in accordance with nature, which according to Seneca is the motto of the Stoic school, you will experience serene interactions with your clients who are themselves operating in accordance with nature.

However, as we all know, the world of business is a competitive place, and you will likely find people like Seneca did, who are corrupt and greedy. In that case, hopefully, you will be doing your daily journaling and negative visualization exercises, which will help you realize when you find the right and the wrong client. Moreover, if it happens that you are dealing with a difficult client, always remember, as we said above, other people do what they do because they think it is for the best. This is one of the things a practicing Stoic must learn to accept. If a client behaves badly towards us—or passes us up for another business, or even betrays us—we must remember, that reflects poorly on *him*. If you have been practicing negative visualization and "pre-mortems," then you should have a plan in place to deal with whatever worst-case scenario a bad client throws at you.

How Stoicism Can Foster Optimal Wellness:

Stoicism is an ideal philosophical practice for limiting harmful stress and anxiety, for learning to control your energy, and for finding balance and managing your time. In fact, its profound connection with mindfulness has led people to call it the Western form of Buddhism. One of the first things to remember when thinking about wellness and Stoicism is that the body is not considered to be under our full control. Obviously, the Stoic discipline would advocate that we do our utmost best to take good care of ourselves. This means we should always strive to eat only healthy foods, to get plenty of vigorous exercises and fresh air and, when we are sick, to seek competent medical treatment (and to follow our trusted doctor's advice!). However, it also recognizes that we can only go so far with our choices about our bodies. As much as we can try to alter our appearance with diet, exercise, cosmetics and clothing, we do not decide how we look when we are born, what strengths or weaknesses our bodies might have, or even if we are born able-bodied or with a severe handicap.

So just remember, every person will have to find his or her own way of dealing with stress, restoring energy, and striving for a balanced life—the Stoics do not spell out a diet or exercise regime. They just establish some basic guidelines for a simple, healthy life that is built around using the minimum necessary. As you try these techniques, do not get angry with yourself if you do not have the desired reaction immediately. Practice having patience with your body as you do with your mental self, and with those around you.

Decreasing Stress: If we practice daily, stoic philosophy is like a built-in de-stress program. Every element of Stoicism teaches us how to decrease stress, because once we truly accept that not everything is in our control—and can distinguish between what is and what is not—a lot of natural stress just melts away. Maybe you were waiting for a major delivery, and a snowstorm hits—let it go! Maybe you were hoping to make a major sale, and the client stopped returning your calls. Did you do everything in your power to convince him to buy from you? Yes? Then let it go. Furthermore, the practice of negative visualization will expose you to stressors—the images of terrible things happening to you and to your loved ones. However, it does so in a controlled environment so that you can react more effectively and with more self-restraint when it comes time to face something that you tried to imagine. Remember, a true Stoic is never surprised, which is a major advantage, because being surprised is one of the worst stressors a human can face.

Increasing Your Energy

One of the great benefits of Stoicism is the way it teaches you to let go of every little thing that does not matter. This means that you can conserve the energy you have previously been wasting on trivial things, and dedicate it to the truly important issues and people in your life. Furthermore, the stoic rituals of evening and morning journaling have been shown to help increase energy in several ways. First, it increases energy because it helps favor restorative sleep: once you have your plan for tomorrow and have let go of today, you will be more likely to fall asleep quickly and sleep more deeply. Second, it increases energy because it gives you a clear plan of action, so you stop wasting valuable energy on making decisions—something psychologists have shown to be very taxing in terms of brain capacity. Third, its emphasis on spending time moving in nature has been proven to be a natural anti-depressant, with just thirty minutes of outdoor time a day having a major boost on people's mood and energy levels.

Finding Your Balance

Stoicism is committed to living in balance with nature. For the founder of Stoicism, Zeno, nature is simply "the way things work." Sounds simple enough. This means that following natural laws is the true meaning of wisdom. Marcus Aurelius wrote: "Philosophy requires only what your nature already demands," which sounds easy enough (until you set out to do it without a proper guide!). Seneca said it like this: "Let us keep to the way which Nature has mapped out for us, and let us not swerve therefrom. If we follow Nature, all is easy and unobstructed; but if we combat Nature, our life differs not a whit from that of men who row against the current." This actually teaches us the true advantage of being balanced and of not excessively striving—although we may fear that by backing off and doing less, we will lose to our competition. Remember that for the Stoics, those who live out of balance with nature are like people rowing their boats upstream, while you will be letting the current take you where it rightly needs to go—and therefore will get there faster and with much less effort.

So, how do we achieve the desired balance that comes from living in accordance with nature? Let's go back to the basic tenets of Stoicism. Above all else, you must only focus on what is within your power. This means to accept your limitations and strengths for what they are. Epictetus had some wise words on this point; he wrote, "If you try to be something you're not or strive for something completely beyond your present capacities, you end up as a pathetic dabbler, trying first to be a wise person, then a bureaucrat, then a politician, then a civic leader. These roles are not consistent. You can't be flying off in countless directions, however appealing they are, and at the same time live an integrated, fruitful life." So think about what is your ultimate goal. Then, plan out the steps to get yourself there, and go through them one by one—do not be a dabbler. Luckily, if you are in harmony with yourself, you will be naturally inclined to pursue a limited number of desires, and you will be free from greed—which is often the feeling that pushes people beyond their natural limits and disturbs their balance.

Making the Most of your Time

The truth is, there are only twenty-four hours in the day, so we have to try to spend them as wisely as possible. Seneca had beautifully accurate words on this point. He wrote, "People are frugal in guarding their personal property; but as soon as it comes to squandering time they are most wasteful of the one thing in which it is right to be stingy." So, are you one of those people? Do you agree to do anything someone asks you because you fear they will not like you or will not give you their business? (If you need some help learning to say no, especially if you are a woman or a minority, Berkshire Hathaway CEO and investor extraordinaire Warren Buffett is very direct on this point: "The difference between successful people and really successful people is that really successful people say no to almost everything.") Do you waste time on tiny minutia, like saving a few pennies here and there? Do you let your mind wander, chasing after pointless worries about things that were not—and will never be—in your control? Do you waste your time on friendships long past their expiration date? Amazon's phenomenally successful founder Jeff Bezos has this to say about friendship: "Life's too short to hang out with people who aren't resourceful." If the answer to any of these questions is yes, then time management is still a major problem for you at this point in the book. In that case, we advise you to review your daily journals and spend a little more time reflecting on your schedule. (See exercise three below for some more helpful tips.)

Practical Advice and Tips for the Stoic Entrepreneur

1. Since seeing things objectively is one of the most important qualities for a Stoic, practice being objective with your employees—and get them to try to be objective with themselves. Schedule a sit-down, face-to-face meeting with each one of your employees. In preparation, ask them to write up a brief, objective summary of their yearly performance, as they feel it would be written from a disinterested outsider. Ask them to evaluate themselves as if they had only observed their performance through a

pane of glass. You do the same: imagine your company was being audited by an external Human Resources firm. Think about how they would describe the performance of every person who works for you. (You can also write one about yourself!) Then during the employee meeting compare the two reviews, and see where you differ in significant ways. Try to brainstorm with them about why that might be. If there are major discrepancies, be sure to schedule a follow-up meeting in order to revisit the issue after a few weeks or months.

2. Plan a retreat with all of your partners, somewhere out of the usual office setting, and preferably out of town and in nature. Ask each person to bring a small, inexpensive gift for the team that symbolizes the way they view the relationship and/or their hopes for it in the future. These gifts could be a small animal, like a lion, that symbolizes courage, pride and resilience, or a hearty plant that reminds the team of its roots. Taking an afternoon to recognize one another, celebrate your interconnectedness, and just take your mind off work for a short period of time, can do wonders to unite a team and bring out the best everyone has to offer.

3. Wellness: time to stop wasting time! Go back to your original journaling exercise where you developed your ideal schedule. Now that you have learned more about the Stoic mentality, ask yourself if the items in your daily schedule are truly in alignment you're your nature. Can you delegate unimportant tasks? What can be automated? What can be discarded? If you are struggling to have healthy meals, try a shopping service or online ordering. Remember, a busy schedule is not necessarily the best schedule (and probably is not). Have you scheduled enough time for exercise and outdoor time? Can you add in a little more, maybe just five minutes per day? How is your sleep schedule? Have you been maintaining important social relations? Have you trimmed away all the friendships that are not serving you? (Remember, time spent on something is time taken away from something else, so be prudent in your choices.)
4. Stoic words of wisdom: now that you have gone through nearly the entire book, go back through it (or through your journal if you have been taking notes on the book) and select your favorite quotation. Use it for the basis of your next morning or evening meditation. (Now that you have almost completed the book, you may want to refer

back to the quotations and intersperse them into your meditations on a regular basis in order to stay connected to what we have learned here.)

5. Bonus challenge: While you are looking through your daily diary entries, consider if anything you have written might be worthy of sharing with the broader public. Ask a trusted friend to look them over and offer his opinion. In the "further reading" section there are references to popular podcasts; there are also countless blogs and even an active Reddit forum on Stoicism. Look through these options and consider reaching out to the hosts or authors to see if they are interested in interviewing you or featuring you as a guest or even a regular co-host. After all, now you have experienced the power of stoicism in your life for at least several months—which means you have taken it more seriously than the majority of people out there who just quote a little phrase here or there to look smart at a party! (Note: this activity is only to be completed *after* reading this entire book! Do not get sidetracked with the publication until its already done.)

One Last Week of Exercises – For Your Entire (Soon-to-be) Stoic Team

Now that you have read the entire book and have taken the time to master each of the stoic teachings and apply them to your own life, it is time to show off your leadership skills and teach your employees to think—and work!—like a stoic.

Look ahead at your next month's calendar. Do not delay any more than that, but scan through your obligations and pick a week that looks conducive to a large, intensive group undertaking. (But do not worry, if you have a lot of employees on the road or clients visiting, etc., all of the exercises can be done individually and remotely. They are designed to help your employees clarify their thinking but *not* take up huge amounts of time.)

Depending on the kind of leader you are and how you communicate with your employees, you may announce the stoic week in an email or in an actual meeting. You may also decide to reveal all seven days at once, or keep them on their toes and give them the challenge just moments before it starts. You know your team best, so you will know what works and does not work for them. (Note: if you have different ideas for a stoic day, feel free to try them out. By now you know the main principles and should feel confident experimenting with them. Remember, stoicism is a growing, changing practice and it needs you to contribute in order to thrive for future generations.)

Day 1: Monday – Teach your employees to start the week off with a morning reflection. Use your experience with your own reflection to guide them in this new endeavor. You can recommend paper or electronic journals, but make sure your employees know that their words are totally private. (You can ask them if they want to raise any related points to you personally, to everyone in a company meeting or on an online collaboration channel, but it should be completely optional.) Give them a few prompts as they start to write, such as: what objectives do you want to achieve today? How do you want to feel at the end of the day? What do you need to do in order to make this day a success? How will you know this day is a success?

But also make sure to encourage them to "clear their throat" to see what emerges when they let themselves be free. Then give them time at the end of the day to do an evening reflection where they evaluate how their day played out and strategize for a successful tomorrow. Ideally, they will want to continue this practice on their own. If you designate ten or fifteen minutes at the start and end of every day, you will be well on your way to helping them for a habit that will make them happier and more productive employees. Try it. It might just be worth way more than twenty or thirty minutes it costs.

Day 2: Tuesday – Prepare your employees to think about the worst-case scenario with some negative visualization exercises. Remember, that the key benefit is to train their rational mind to remain in charge of their powerful emotions, allowing them to stay calm and self-controlled if and when something goes awry at work. If they regularly practice negative visualization, your employees will hone their ability to scrutinize a problem and understand every single aspect of it. Tell them to focus on their biggest project at work, and to imagine every single part going wrong. Ask them to think about how it makes them feel. Then, ask them to write down two or three things they could do to prevent or improve this worst-case scenario. Allow them time during the day to create a back-up plan. Remember, you are investing in your own future by giving them this valuable time right now.

Day 3: Wednesday – Teach your employees to reframe their negative perceptions. Using the results of the journaling and the negative visualization, ask your employees to come up with as many silver linings as they possibly can fathom. Ask them: what went "wrong" in their day? Then challenge them to separate the parts that were under their control and the parts that were external to them. How did they handle the parts under their control? Remind them that is where the true good and evil of any situation lies. Another reminder: this is all training for a future experience. Every single person makes mistakes, but the truly successful people learn from their mistakes and change their future behavior. Make sure this exercise does not become a blame game amongst employees by insisting that everyone recognize his or her responsibility. Tell them that these writings will be kept private, so no one fears creating a climate of suspicion.

Day 4: Thursday – Increase productivity! Tell your employees to look through their schedule and then prepare a short analysis of how they are spending their time (good preparatory activity for this day is to have them use a time tracking app for a week – there are many free ones available online). Ask them to meet with you or their immediate supervisor (obviously, this will take longer if you have a lot of employees, so plan accordingly) to review how they are spending their time. See where they can cut out, automate or delegate items that are less important. Try to see if they have been putting off a meaningful project because of busywork. Or better yet, see if they can find it themselves. Remember, you are teaching them to be resourceful so that you can better spend your time elaborating on your company's developing vision.

Day 5: Friday – Take responsibility. Today is the end of the workweek, and it is time for your employees to look inside themselves in relation to their whole team and to figure out their role in the complex team dynamics. Have the contributed as fully as they should have? Why or why not? Have they behaved with dignity and in alignment with company values? Why or why not? Make sure this is not perceived as a punishment or an attempt at spying. Just ask them to reflect on these stoic principles and to make sure they are acknowledging their responsibility for what is under their control and the choices they make.

Day 6: Saturday – Take a break! Remember, the Stoics are about productivity, efficiency, motivation and action. But this is only possible if you fully disconnect on a regular basis. This might sound totally counterintuitive, but the boldest move you could make for this Saturday activity is to tell your employees to unplug. Tell them not to check their work email for a whole day. (Did that make you nervous? Relax! Do a negative visualization. What could possibly happen in just twenty-four hours without email...?) Encourage them to take a walk in nature, go for a bike ride, or to take a swim with their friends. Tell them to spend time on self-care, talking to family, eating a good meal, and connecting to what they truly love. Trust us, they will thank you for it on Monday!

Day 7: Sunday – Time to look back on the whole week. As your employees to write another journal entry (hopefully by now they are enjoying the process). Ask them how the stoic week changed their life. Did it meet their expectations? Did it change some aspect of their work-life or their home life? Why or why not? Did a certain principle resonate with them? Was one principle harder for them to work with? Why do they think that is? Consider using the results of this activity in a group meeting, again, only if people feel comfortable sharing. If they do, you will have a rich source of information about the people around you, which can only improve your leadership abilities. If not, make sure they know that this is okay and that there will not be any negative repercussions from you.

Bonus: Collect your favorite stoic quotations from this book and use them as the basis of a daily email message to your team. This will help make these principles even more concrete and powerful. Ask your employees to comment on them with one another or to discover their own quotations to help them succeed.

Summary: The Chapter In Brief

Using the umbrella concept of *sympatheia,* chapter 6 offered advice about a range of different business relationships, including employees, business partners, and clients. It also took a deeper look at negotiation and selling tactics for the stoic entrepreneur. Then, it had practical advice about individual wellness and how stoicism can teach you to conserve energy, decrease stress, and improve your time management skills. Finally, it concluded with a series of exercises, including a stoic week to lead your employees through at work.

Chapter 6: Conclusion: What the Stoics Can Teach Us about Obtaining and Maintaining Success in Business

> "There are two of the most immediately useful thoughts you will dip into. First that things cannot touch the mind: they are external and inert; anxieties can only come from your internal judgment. Second, that all these things you see will change almost as you look at them, and then will be no more. Constantly bring to mind all that you yourself have already seen changed. The universe is change: life is judgement."
>
> -Marcus Aurelius

If you have read the book all the way through to this point (thank you! And congratulations!), you are probably able to understand this quotation by Marcus Aurelius by yourself and what it means from a Stoic perspective. But in case you want one more quick explanation, remember that for the Stoics, it is not an actual event that makes us happy or miserable, but the way we interpret it. As Epictetus puts it, "Men are disturbed not by events but by their opinion about events." So as you go through the stages of your business, whether as a sole proprietor or as the CEO of a fledgling startup, it is crucial not to just react to outside events. If you do, it is easy to slip into a feeling that life is treating you unfairly—and from there, to fall into a resigned depression that will only make things worse. After all, no matter how bad something is, remember that it will soon be over, as with all things in life, including your life itself.

Here, we see Stoicism overlap with Buddhism, an Eastern philosophy that emphasizes the impermanence of life and the transitory nature of existence. If you remember that desiring a certain outcome is a lose-lose proposition, you will know not to waste your short, precious life in search of worldly goods. The most important thing to pursue that will give you true happiness is a virtue because it sets you free from the chains of endless desire. Epictetus was actually a slave, and thanks to the teachings of Stoicism, he was able to live a fulfilling life. No wonder historian Paul Veyne described Stoicism like this: "Stoicism is not so much an ethic as it is a paradoxical recipe for happiness."

Take Away Lessons from This Book:

Chapter 1 and Chapter 2 introduced you to the two key exercises of stoicism: daily journaling and negative visualization. Journaling—morning and evening reflections—

help you to achieve a clear vision and to learn important lessons from what you have done, whether good or bad, success or failure. On the subject of success and failure, try taking the advice of Microsoft founder and philanthropist Bill Gates "It's fine to celebrate success but it is more important to heed the lessons of failure." While journaling needs to be done every day to really have an impact, negative visualization, on the other hand, does not have to be a daily practice. It can be performed whenever you are about to embark on a new, intimidating event. Remember, the repeated exposure to negative imagery actually numbs you to it, and this makes it possible for you to bravely confront your worst fears—and to prepare for them in advance, so you'll never be surprised or caught off guard. It also reminds you that life is short, that everything is borrowed, and to appreciate what you have. Do not make a mountain out of a molehill!

Chapter 3 got you down into the trenches and told you about the value of decisive action. Once you make a decision and set the wheels in motion, the stoics then give valuable, practical advice about increasing motivation by remembering the uncertainty of life (do not forget: you could be dead tomorrow, so stop procrastinating and get to work!). They teach us to have intense discipline, and that includes mastering your emotions. It also means a Stoic cane endure pain without complaint and can push himself as hard as he can possibly go, and then pushes a little harder. At the same time, Stoic philosophy respects time for rest too. And it tells us about ideal ways to optimize your productivity by delegating, automating and letting go of the things that do not matter (because every person's time is limited!). Finally, when a project is finished, remember that a stoic leader takes ownership of any results, good or bad, and he perseveres through any challenges that he and his team will inevitably face.

Chapter 4 told you about the power of introspection and extrospection in influencing your life and work an entrepreneur. While it is important to know yourself profoundly, remember you do not exist in a vacuum. This means you also must objectively study those around you and strive to surround yourself with only the best people—that is, the people who bring out the best in you and help you live according to your virtue. Of course, you must know your friends, but knowing your fellow businessmen and women (and how you will react to them) will provide you with an advantage when it comes to negotiating. In the end, however, the best result is one that goes along with nature and honors our interconnectedness. A compromise that respects both parties is always the best outcome.

Chapter 5 introduced to you the concept of *sympatheia* (interconnectedness) in order to give advice about how to improve various essential business relationships. It talks about how to handle your employees, especially if they are not performing. It also discusses the important role of developing good relationships with your business partners, which means knowing how to talk and listen to them from a Stoic perspective. Then, it gives you important advice about how to attract, maintain and troubleshoot problems with clients, especially in the early stages of growing your business. Then, it also takes a deeper look at negotiation and selling tactics for the stoic entrepreneur. Thanks to its emphasis on the fleeting nature of life, stoicism also has practical advice about personal wellness. By teaching people to focus on what truly matters and what they can actually control, stoicism teaches people how to conserve their precious energy, decrease anxiety, obtain balance and improve their time management skills. This chapter asked *you* to become a teacher, giving you a series of easy, practical and powerful exercises to give your team a week of stoicism at work.

We hope you enjoyed this introduction to Stoicism and entrepreneurship, and that in the process of reading, you have found inspiration and actionable advice that you can put to work for the benefit of yourself, of your business endeavors and of those around you. Remember, Stoicism is not an all or nothing proposition, even if the ancient Stoic seem like towering icons of perfection. It's not that you're either completely Stoic, or you're not Stoic at all. Stoicism is not about criticizing or evaluating how Stoic someone is, and it is not just for the mythical "sage." Stoics themselves recognized the value of the *prokopton*, the person who is "making progress." This sense of progress does not typically follow a straight line. Instead, as the Stoics themselves tell us repeatedly, it is all about getting back up after you have been thrown down by life. If you take even the quickest read through the classic Stoic literature, you will see that failure is an accepted part of the process, so as you are reaching the end of this book, commit to returning regularly to its principles, so that you can make that most important of commitments, the commitment to improve yourself, no matter how long it takes. After all, when you start a new exercise routine in order to get into better shape, you would never start by trying to lift the same amount of weight or running the same distance as the people who have been training for years. You take stock of your current physical fitness, you assess your weaknesses and past experiences, and you start out with a lighter amount of weight or a shorter distance. And then you keep on going. Eventually you can start to increase the amount of weight, to run farther, and you take on new exercises, and eventually sign up for a marathon. Keep this same principle in mind as you continue your journey as a *prokopton,* and make sure to practice and develop your temperance, your self-control as you embrace this life-changing discipline.

Finally, we leave you with a few powerful reflections. One that is particularly resonant is Marcus Aurelius' thoughts on why you should get started today and live the stoic lifestyle described in this book. He writes: **"Remember how long you have been putting this off, how many extensions the gods gave you, and you didn't use them. At some point you have to recognize what the world it is that you belong to; what power rules it and from what source you spring; That there is a limit to the time assigned you, and if you do not use it to free yourself, it will be gone and will never return." Epictetus also has a compelling exhortation to any of you who are still hesitating about getting started. He writes,** "Now is the time to get serious about living your ideals. How long can you afford to put off who you really want to be? Your nobler self cannot wait any longer. Put your principles into practice – now. Stop the excuses and procrastination. This is your life! […] Decide to be extraordinary and do what you need to do – now."

Now if that's not inspiration to stop reading and get to work, we do not know what is!

Further Reading

Today, stoicism is an incredibly popular topic, and no wonder, if you stop and consider all the successful world leaders who profess their allegiance to the stoic world view. Check out these resources to get more information about stoicism and learn how it can apply to your everyday life:

For general background, we recommend that you try the first introduction to stoic philosophy published in recent years:

Stoicism by John Sellars (2014)

Or: Stoicism: A Very Short Introduction by Brad Inwood (2018)

For more information on Marcus Aurelius, you should try:

The Inner Citadel (2001) and Philosophy as a Way of Life (1995) by Pierre Hadot

Marcus Aurelius by Matthew Arnold (essay)

For more information on Cato, you should try:

Rome's Last Citizen: The Life and Legacy of Cato, Mortal Enemy of Caesar by Rob Goodman and Jimmy Son (2014)

Cato the Younger by Plutarch and John Dryde (2013)

For practical applications of stoicism in today's modern world, you should check out:

The Daily Stoic: 366 Meditations on Wisdom, Perseverance, and the Art of Living

By Ryan Holiday, Stephen Hanselman (2016)

How to Be a Stoic: Using Ancient Philosophy to Live a Modern Life

By Massimo Pigliucci (2017)

The Practicing Stoic: A Philosophical User's Manual, by Ward Farnsworth (2018)

Stoicism and the Art of Happiness: Practical wisdom for everyday life: embrace perseverance, strength and happiness with stoic philosophy by Donald Robertson (2018)

Stoicism: A Stoic Approach to Modern Life by Tom Miles (2015)

A Guide to the Good Life: The Ancient Art of Stoic Joy, By William B. Irvine (2008)

For a memoir of true stoics who mastered themselves and beat the odds, you should try:

Can't Hurt Me by David Goggins (2018)

Or: Courage Under Fire: Testing Epictetus's Doctrines in a Laboratory of Human Behavior by James Stockdale (1993)

For original writings by Greek stoics, try the following:

Meditations by Marcus Aurelius

Letters from a Stoic by Seneca

On The Shortness of Life by Seneca

Discourses and Selected Writings by Epictetus

Fragments by Heraclitus

If you want a digital assistant to help you deepen your connection to stoicism—and provide a daily reminder to complete your practices, you should try the following top-rated apps:

Stoic Meditations, produced by the Stoa Nova in partnership with Adam Musial-Bright (currently available on the iTunes store, no Android version available). The meditations allow you to start your morning with a stoic thought and to perform Stoic self-improvement activities.

Stoic: Self Reflect Journaling is a free, top-rated app developed by Maciej Lobodinzski to help you learn to cope with stress and to start truly enjoying your life. It contains a morning and evening routine, reflective exercises, history, philosophy and wisdom. There is a premium subscription option.

Daily Stoic, developed by Brass Check, provides daily quotes from Marcus Aurelius, Seneca, Epictetus and others.

Stoic Library provides the most important classical stoic texts, including Marcus Aurelius, Seneca, Epictetus and others, in one convenient place.

Stoa is a meditation app for practitioners and doers. It has 2+ hours of guided meditations to help you embrace the stoic disciplines and apply them to your life.

Stoicism is now a popular topic for podcasts, so you can continue to learn about it while you are driving or exercising. You should check out:

The Tim Ferriss Show

Host: Tim FerrissWebsite: https://tim.blog/tag/stoicism/

Tim Ferris talks about a range of topics, including stoicism and how it applies to Ferriss' life and work.

The Practical Stoic Podcast

Hosted by: Simon DrewWebsite: http://www.risetothegoodlife.com/practicalstoicpodcast/

Topic: The Practical Stoic Podcast features concrete advice from the ancient Stoic philosophers.

Stoic Mettle

Hosted by: Scott Hebert Website: https://stoicmettle.com/

These podcasts are generally short and practical, with advice that is easy to put into action. He uses his personal life to teach Stoic ideas and interviews contemporary Stoics to ask them to contribute further insights.

Stoic Meditations

Hosted by: Massimo Pigliucci Website: https://anchor.fm/stoicmeditations

(For more from Pigliucci see the book **How To Be A Stoic** and the Stoic Meditations app above). A Professor of Philosophy at CUNY-City College, Massimo Pigliucci's Stoic Meditations are comprised of short readings from the ancient Stoics, with his scholarly commentary that makes them easy to understand in a modern context. Try adding it to your daily routine!

Good Fortune

Hosted by: Matt van Natta Website: https://immoderatestoic.com/good-fortune/

Topic: Van Natta does readings of stoic texts and interprets them in the context of modern-day life.

Stoic Philosophy Podcast

Hosted by: Justin VaculaWebsite: http://justinvacula.com/

The Stoic Philosophy Podcast offers practical tidbits for daily living. It explores a broad set of topics that are relatable to everyday contemporary life.

The Sunday Stoic Podcast

Hosted by: Steve KarafiatWebsite: https://sundaystoic.wixsite.com/home

Sunday Stoic is a podcast that focuses on readings of the ancient Stoics with modern applications of their most salient lessons.

www.ingramcontent.com/pod-product-compliance
Lightning Source LLC
Chambersburg PA
CBHW072019110526
44592CB00012B/1373